© 2013 by B&H Publishing Group
Nashville, Tennessee

Scripture quotations are taken from
the Holman Christian Standard Bible®,
Copyright © 1999, 2000, 2002, 2003, 2009
by Holman Bible Publishers.

ISBN: 978-1-4336-8044-1
Dewey Decimal Classification: J220.95
Subject Heading: BIBLE STORIES \ SALVATION \ CHRISTIAN LIFE

2 3 4 5 6 7 8 • 17 16 15 14 13

# THE BIG PICTURE INTERACTIVE BIBLE STORYBOOK

B&H KIDS

Nashville, Tennessee

# A Letter to Parents

**A** strong foundation in the Word of God is the most important thing you can leave for your kids. You want your children to know not only the Bible, but also the God who has revealed Himself to us in its pages. The prayer of our hearts is that through the work of the Spirit, God would use His Word to introduce our kids to Jesus. It's a message that we want to give them at home, as well as in the church.

There are all sorts of Bible storybooks on the shelf today, but not all storybooks are equal. Many Bible stories are presented to kids in a way that seems to communicate the primary message: "be good."

What sometimes gets lost in the journey through Bible stories is the good news of what Christ has done to save the lost. In other words, when we focus on reinforcing good behavior, we may be missing the heart-change brought about by the gospel. Even worse, we condition our kids to think that the Bible is all about them.

*This Bible storybook is different.* Here are some of the things you will find here:

## 1. A supplement to the Bible that focuses on the big story

First, you'll see that this book is designed to supplement Bible reading by showing how the Bible stories connect to form one big story. Why is this important?

Well, when we take Bible stories out of context to glean moral lessons from them, we can leave kids with the impression that the Bible is much like Aesop's Fables—interesting tales with moral application.

Even though the Bible has moral application and does give us some terrific stories, it actually tells one overarching story. These stories fit together. They tell us the story of our world—where we've come from and where we are going.

We believe it's important that children recognize how these Bible stories are connected. That's why these stories are presented chronologically.

## 2. Questions that focus our attention on God

Once we recognize that the Bible as a whole is telling us a great story, we discover that we are not the main characters. The Bible is first and foremost about God. He is the hero.

These stories provide us with life application, yes. But before we get to application, we ought to ask, "What does this story tell us about God? What attributes and characteristics of God are on display in this story? If the Bible's big story is about God's bringing about the redemption of His fallen world, then what picture of God do we see in the smaller stories?"

You'll see that these stories include Big Picture Questions and Answers. These are designed to help kids understand the truths about God, humanity, sin, and redemption—truths we learn in the Bible through the telling of these stories.

## 3. Connections that point us to Jesus

Just because you know the Bible doesn't mean the Word will bear fruit in your life. It is possible to know the Scriptures, read the Scriptures, revere the Scriptures, and study the Scriptures and miss the point entirely. Jesus told the Jewish leaders of the day that even though they had meticulous knowledge of the Old Testament, they had missed the truth that the Old Testament is ultimately about Him.

Whenever we study the stories of the Bible, we need to ask how they point us to Christ. The reason God's Word changes our life is not because of our personal study but because in the Scriptures we are introduced to Jesus, the Author.

That's why we've included "Christ Connections" for every Bible story. These connections are just one way to help you as a parent show how every story is pointing to Christ and His work for us.

## Why this book?

"Be good" is not the message of the Bible. "Be saved" is. We want our children to know that God is good, and He is the hero who sent His Son to die for our sins.

Biblical behavior should not flow from obligation and compulsion. God cares about our hearts. Our hearts are not changed by the commands of the Law. Our hearts are changed when they overflow with love for the Savior. As we experience the grace of what God has done for us in Christ, our hearts are free to worship and obey. It's important that, when giving our children these commands, we also show them how the Holy Spirit, through the gospel, gives them the strength to obey these commands.

So, enjoy the big story of the Bible and introduce your children to the God who loved us in this way: "He gave His One and Only Son, so that everyone who believes in Him will not perish but have eternal life" (John 3:16).

# Parent Connection

## Remember:

*The grass withers, the flowers fade, but the word of our God remains forever.* —Isaiah 40:8

## Read:

John 1:1–18 really puts the big picture of the Bible in perspective. From the beginning of the world to this very moment, God has had a plan. His is a perfect plan of sacrifice and grace to illustrate His unending, undying love for His children. Sometimes the picture may seem too big to understand, but as you study story by story, piece by piece, the puzzle will come together and reveal God's big-picture plan for your life.

## Think:

1. Name two or three Bible stories that seem to fit together.
2. What did the people in these stories learn about God?
3. What do these stories all have in common?
4. How are they different?
5. How are these stories similar to and different from your own story?
6. What has your story taught you about God?

## Do:

Show how it all ties together. Create a big-picture poster.
1. Ask an adult for a poster board. You can also use a large piece of paper.
2. In the center draw a symbol that represents God. You can use a cross, a heart, the word God, or whatever God means to you.
3. Above that, draw another symbol or illustration that represents another story from the Bible.
4. Draw a line to connect that story symbol to God. Then on the line, write a characteristic of God—or something you learned about God—from that story.
5. As you continue to read the Word of God, add stories to your big picture. Hang the poster where you can see it, and take some time to look back at the stories you've read and what they've taught you about God and His big picture.

*If your big picture is not perfectly clear, don't worry.*
*Keep seeking God through His Word, and He will continue to reveal Himself to you.*

## Bonus Material: Bring the Bible to Life!

Watch the Bible stories come alive in this first-of-its-kind *Interactive Bible Storybook* by downloading the FREE Augmented Realty app from B&H Kids. Narrations by Jenna Lucado pull readers in to see 145 full-color illustrations jumping right off the page. Plus, QR codes throughout connect to videos featuring key Bible stories.

### DOWNLOAD THE FREE APP NOW

Scan this QR code or search in the app store for "B&H Kids AR." Then it's as easy as 1, 2, 3 . . .

**1** Scan any icon

**2** Scan the illustration

**3** Watch it come to life!

**Super Bonus!** Look for QR codes throughout the stories.
Scan them with any QR code reader for bonus Bible story videos!

**HEY PARENTS!**

*Parents:* By scanning this icon with the AR App, you can download a complete data set for *The Big Picture Interactive Bible Storybook* to your device, and can then use the app off-line. This may take some time depending on your connection.

# The Big Picture Bible Storybook: Icons

*These icons are divided topically across the stories and designed to match The Gospel Project for Kids curriculum plan.*

## In the Beginning: Creation and the Patriarchs

God's story began with creation. When sin entered the world, God set in motion His plan to redeem His people through His Son, Jesus Christ—a descendant of Abraham.

## A Nation Is Born: Moses and the Israelites

The exodus was the greatest act of redemption in the Old Testament. One day God would send His Son, Jesus, to rescue His people from a greater slavery to sin and death.

## Life in the Land: Joshua and the Judges

When God's people entered the promised land, God raised up judges to deliver them from their enemies. Hundreds of years later, Jesus came as the ultimate and final Savior.

## A Kingdom Creation: Ruth, Samuel, and the Early Kings

The people of Israel rejected God as their leader. God gave them a king. Through this line of kings, God would one day bring the true and final King: His Son, Jesus.

## Trouble at the Top: Sin and Israel's Fall

God sent prophets to warn the Israelites of His coming judgment on their sin. The prophets also gave messages of hope. The prophet Isaiah told of a servant, Jesus, who would suffer so we could be forgiven.

## Exile: Judah and the Exile

Despite the warnings of several prophets, the Southern Kingdom of Judah was judged for their sin and exiled. The prophet Ezekiel told of a future hope—of a God who can make dead people alive through His Son, Jesus.

## Faithful Followers: Daniel and the Exiles Return

Daniel remained faithful to God during captivity in Babylon. God saved His people from physical captivity as He would one day send Jesus to save and restore His people from spiritual captivity.

## The Promised One: Jerusalem Rebuilt, John the Baptist, and Jesus' Early Years

God restored a remnant and reminded them of His promise of a new covenant through Jesus. God sent His Son into the world to save His people from their sin.

## Jesus' Ministry Begins: Jesus' Sermons and Healings

Jesus was revealed as the fulfillment of Scripture, the promised Messiah. His teachings and healings showed His authority and power as the Son of God.

## Power and Parables: The Parables of Jesus

Jesus demonstrated His power over the brokenness of the world. He taught in parables so His followers would understand how to live in anticipation of His Second Coming.

## Jesus Saves: Jesus Provided Our Sacrifice

Jesus lived the perfect life we cannot live and died the guilty death we don't want to die. On the third day, God raised Him from the dead. Jesus saves sinners who trust in Him.

## The Church: Paul, the Church, and the Return of Christ

The church is God's plan to bring praise and glory to Jesus. One day, Jesus will come back to earth. He will undo every bad thing caused by sin, and those who trust in Him will be with Him and enjoy Him forever.

# Bible Stories of the Old Testament

God Created the World and People: Genesis 1–2 .................................................................... 2

Sin Entered the World: Genesis 3–4 ...................................................................................... 4

Noah and the Ark: Genesis 6:5–9:17 ...................................................................................... 6

The Tower of Babel: Genesis 9:1; 11:1–9 ............................................................................... 8

Job: Job 1–42 .......................................................................................................................... 10

God's Promise to Abraham: Genesis 12:2–3; 15:1–21 .......................................................... 12

The Sons of Abraham: Genesis 16:1–16; 17:1–9, 15–22; 21:1–7 ........................................ 14

God Tested Abraham: Genesis 22:1–19 ................................................................................. 16

God Remembered His Promise: Genesis 25:19–26; 26:1–6; 28:10–22 ................................ 18

The Stolen Blessing: Genesis 25:27–34; 27:1–45 ................................................................. 20

Jacob's New Name: Genesis 31:3; 32–33 .............................................................................. 22

Joseph Sent to Egypt: Genesis 37:1–36; 39:1–41:57 ............................................................ 24

Joseph's Dreams Came True: Genesis 41:53–46:34; 50:15–21 ............................................ 26

Moses Was Born and Called: Exodus 1:6–2:10, 23–25; 3:1–4:20 ....................................... 28

Moses Confronted Pharaoh: Exodus 5:1–6:13; 6:28–11:1 ................................................... 30

The Passover: Exodus 11:1–13:16 .......................................................................................... 32

The Israelites Crossed the Red Sea: Exodus 13:17–17:7 ...................................................... 34

The Ten Commandments: Exodus 19:1–20:21; 31:18; 32:1–35; 34:1–9 .............................. 36

The Tabernacle Was Built: Exodus 25:8; 35:4–40:38 ............................................................ 38

God Gave Rules for Sacrifice: Leviticus 1–27 ...................................................................... 40

Joshua and Caleb: Numbers 13:1–14:38 ............................................................................... 42

The Bronze Snake: Numbers 16:1–3; 17:1–12; 20:1–12, 14–20; 21:4–9 ............................ 44

Balaam: Numbers 22:1–24:25 ............................................................................................... 46

The Israelites Crossed the Jordan River: Joshua 1:1; 3–4 ................................................... 48

The Conquest of Jericho: Joshua 2; 6 ................................................................................... 50

Achan Sinned: Joshua 7 ......................................................................................................... 52

The Defeat of Ai: Joshua 8 ..................................................................................................... 54

The Day the Sun Stood Still: Joshua 9; 10:1–15 ................................................................... 56

Joshua Spoke to the People: Joshua 23:1–24:28 .................................................................. 58

The First Judges Judges: 3:7–31 ............................................................................................ 60

Deborah and Barak: Judges 4–5 ............................................................................................ 62

Gideon: Judges 6–8 ................................................................................................................ 64

Samson: Judges 13–16 ........................................................................................................... 66

Ruth and Boaz: Ruth 1–4 ....................................................................................................... 68

Eli and Boy Samuel: 1 Samuel 1–3 ....................................................................................... 70

The Ark Was Captured: 1 Samuel 4–5 .................................................................................. 72

Israel Demanded a King: 1 Samuel 8–10 .............................................................................. 74

God Rejected Saul as King: 1 Samuel 13:1–14; 14:18–48; 15:1–35 .................................... 76

David and Goliath: 1 Samuel 16–17 ...................................................................................... 78

David and Jonathan: 1 Samuel 18:1–11; 19:1–7; 20:1–42 ................................................... 80

God's Covenant with David: 2 Samuel 7 .............................................................................. 82

David Sinned and Was Restored: 2 Samuel 11:1–12:14; Psalm 51 ..............................84
Solomon Asked for Wisdom: 1 Kings 2:1–4,10–12; 3:1–15 ..............................86
Solomon Built the Temple: 1 Kings 6:1–8:66 ..............................88
King Solomon's Sin Divided the Kingdom: 1 Kings 11–12 ..............................90
Poetry and Wisdom: Psalms, Proverbs, Ecclesiastes (select passages) ..............................92
Israel's History of Evil Kings: 1 Kings 16 ..............................94
Elijah Confronted Evil Ahab: 1 Kings 17:1; 18 ..............................96
Elijah Ran from Jezebel: 1 Kings 19 ..............................98
Elisha and Naaman: 2 Kings 5 ..............................100
The Northern Kingdom Was Destroyed: 2 Kings 17:1–23 ..............................102
Amos, Prophet to Israel: Amos 1–9 ..............................104
Hosea, Prophet to Israel: Hosea 1–14 ..............................106
Jonah, Prophet to Nineveh: Jonah 1–4 ..............................108
Joel, Prophet to Judah: Joel 1–3 ..............................110
God Called Isaiah: Isaiah 6 ..............................112
Isaiah Confronted King Ahaz: Isaiah 7 ..............................114
Hezekiah, Judah's Faithful King: 2 Kings 18–20 ..............................116
Isaiah Preached about the Messiah: Isaiah 53 ..............................118
Micah, Prophet to Judah: Micah 1–7 ..............................120
Josiah's Reforms: 2 Chronicles 34–35 ..............................122
Zephaniah, Prophet to Judah: Zephaniah 1–3 ..............................124
Habakkuk, Prophet to Judah: Habakkuk 1–3 ..............................126
Nahum, Prophet to Nineveh: Nahum 1–3 ..............................128
God Called Jeremiah: Jeremiah 1 ..............................130
Jeremiah Warned of God's Judgment: Jeremiah 36 ..............................132
Judah Was Taken into Captivity: 2 Chronicles 36:1–21 ..............................134
Ezekiel Prophesied to the Exiles: Ezekiel 10 ..............................136
Ezekiel and the Dry Bones: Ezekiel 37 ..............................138
Daniel and His Friends Obeyed God: Daniel 1 ..............................140
Shadrach, Meshach, and Abednego: Daniel 3 ..............................142
God Gave Daniel Wisdom: Daniel 5 ..............................144
Daniel Was Rescued from the Lions: Daniel 6 ..............................146
Obadiah the Prophet: Obadiah 1–9 ..............................148
Zerubbabel Led the Captives Home: Ezra 1:1–2:2; 2:64–3:13 ..............................150
Haggai, Prophet to Judah: Haggai 1–2 ..............................152
Zechariah, Prophet to Judah: Zechariah 1–14 ..............................154
The Temple Was Completed: Ezra 4:24–6:22 ..............................156
Esther Saved Her People: Esther 4:1–5:14; 7:1–10 ..............................158
Nehemiah Heard News of Jerusalem: Nehemiah 1–2 ..............................160
Jerusalem's Walls Rebuilt: Nehemiah 3:1–6:16 ..............................162
Ezra Read the Law: Nehemiah 8:1–12 ..............................164
Malachi the Prophet: Malachi 1–4 ..............................166

# Bible Stories of the New Testament

The Family of Jesus: Matthew 1:1–17; Luke 3:23–38 ....................................................170
John's Birth Was Predicted: Luke 1:5–25 ...................................................................172
Prophets Told About Jesus' Birth: Isaiah 7:1–14; 9:1–7; 11:1–5; Micah 5:2........................174
Angels Spoke to Mary and Joseph: Luke 1:26–56; Matthew 1:18–24..................................176
Mary Visited Elizabeth: Luke 1:39–56 ........................................................................178
John the Baptist Was Born: Luke 1:57–80.....................................................................180
Jesus Was Born: Luke 2:1–20 ....................................................................................182
Jesus Was Dedicated: Luke 2:21–40 ...........................................................................184
The Wise Men Visited Jesus: Matthew 2:1–21 ..............................................................186
Jesus at the Temple: Luke 2:41–52..............................................................................188
Jesus Was Baptized: Matthew 3:1–6; 13–17; Mark 1:9–11; Luke 3:21–22.............................190
Jesus Was Tempted: Matthew 4:1–11; Luke 4:1–13; Mark 1:12, 13 ....................................192
Jesus Called His Disciples: Matthew 4:18–22; 9:9–13; Mark 1:16–20; 2:13–14; 3:13–19;
    Luke 5:27–32; 6:12–16 .........................................................................................194
Jesus Met Nicodemus: John 3:1–21 .............................................................................196
Jesus and John the Baptist: John 3:22–36 .....................................................................198
Jesus Met a Samaritan Woman: John 4:1–26 ................................................................200
Jesus Returned to Nazareth: Luke 4:16–30 ...................................................................202
Jesus Healed an Official's Son: John 4:46–54 ................................................................204
Jesus Drove Out Unclean Spirits: Mark 1:21–28; Luke 4:31–37........................................206
Jesus Healed Peter's Mother-in-Law: Matthew 8:14–17; Mark 1:29–31; Luke 4:38–39 ..........208
Jesus Cleansed a Leper: Matthew 8:1–4; Mark 1:35–45; Luke 5:12–16................................210
Four Friends Helped: Matthew 9:1–8; Mark 2:1–12; Luke 5:17–26 ....................................212
Jesus Healed a Man's Hand: Matthew 12:9–14; Mark 3:1–6; Luke 6:6–11 ...........................214
The Sermon on the Mount: Matthew 5–7 .....................................................................216
Parable of the Sower: Matthew 13:1–23; Mark 4:1–20; Luke 8 .........................................218
The Lost Parables: Luke 15 .......................................................................................220
Jesus Calmed the Storm: Matthew 8:23–27; Mark 4:35–41; Luke 8:22–25............................222
Jesus Fed Five Thousand: Matthew 14:13–21; Mark 6:30–44; Luke 9:10–17; John 6:1–14.............224
Jesus Healed a Blind Man: Matthew 20:29–34; Mark 10:46–52; Luke 18:35–43 .....................226
Jesus Drove Out Demons: Matthew 8:28–34; Mark 5:1–20; Luke 8:26–39 ...........................228
Jesus Had Power Over Death: John 11:1–44....................................................................230
Parable of the Vineyard Workers: Matthew 20:1–16 .......................................................232
Parable of the Wedding Feast: Matthew 22:1–14 ...........................................................234
Parable of the Faithful Servant: Matthew 24:45–51; Luke 12:42–48....................................236
Parable of the Rich Man and Lazarus: Luke 16:19–31......................................................238
Parable of the Talents: Matthew 25:14–30; Luke 19:11–27 ...............................................240
The Rich Young Ruler: Mark 10:17–34; Luke 18:18–33 ...................................................242
Jesus Was Anointed: Matthew 26:6–13; Mark 14:3–9; John 12:1–8 ....................................244
The Triumphal Entry: Matthew 21:1–11; Mark 11:1–11; Luke 19:28–44; John 12:12–19......246
Jesus Cleansed the Temple: Matthew 21:12–17; Mark 11:15–19; Luke 19:45–48; John 2:13–16...248

The Widow's Gift: Mark 12:41–44; Luke 21:1–4.........................................................250

Preparation for Passover: Matthew 26:17–19; Mark 14:12–16; Luke 22:7–13 ........................252

The Last Supper: Matthew 26:20–30; Mark 14:17–26; Luke 22:14–23; John 13:21–30...........254

Jesus' Crucifixion and Resurrection: Matthew 26:36–28:10 ......................................256

The Emmaus Disciples: Mark 16:12–13; Luke 24:13–35.............................................258

Jesus Appeared to the Disciples: Mark 16:14; Luke 24:36–43; John 20:19–29; Acts 1:3 .........260

Jesus Served Breakfast by the Sea: John 21:1–14.....................................................262

Jesus Gave the Great Commission: Matthew 28:18–20; Mark 16:15–18 ..................................264

Jesus Ascended to Heaven: Acts 1:4–11 ....................................................................266

The Holy Spirit Came: Acts 2:1–46 ..........................................................................268

The Church Met Needs: Acts 3:1–10; 4:32–37..........................................................270

Seven Men Were Chosen: Acts 1:23–26; 6:1–7..........................................................272

Stephen's Address: Acts 6:8–7:60............................................................................274

Saul on the Road to Damascus: Acts 8:1–3; 9:1–31 ...................................................276

Paul's First Journey: Acts 13:1–15:35 ......................................................................278

Paul's Second Journey: Acts 15:36–16:40 ................................................................280

Paul Preached in Europe: Acts 15:36–16:40............................................................282

Paul's Third Journey: Acts 18:18–21:16 ...................................................................284

Paul's Ministry to Rome: Acts 21:17–28:31............................................................286

Church Responsibility: 1 Corinthians 1–16.............................................................288

Christ's Return Was Predicted: 2 Thessalonians 1–3 ................................................290

God's Warning to Seven Churches: Revelation 1–3...................................................292

Jesus Christ Will Return: Revelation 19–22.............................................................294

# Bible Stories of The Old Testament

# God Created the World and People  Genesis 1-2

In the beginning, there was only God. Then God created the heavens and the earth. But the earth had no shape, and it was dark and empty.

God said, "Let there be light!" and there was light. God separated the light from the dark. He called the light "day" and the darkness "night." This was the first day of creation.

God then said, "Let the waters be separated." So God created a great space between the waters on the earth and the waters above the earth. He called the space "sky." This was the second day of creation.

God said, "Let the water under the sky be gathered into one place, and let dry land appear." God called the dry land "earth" and the waters "seas." God then said, "Let the earth grow plants and trees." The plants and trees grew, and God saw that they were good. This was the third day of creation.

Next God said, "Let there be lights in the sky to separate the day from the night." So God made the sun to shine during the day and the moon and stars to shine at night. This was the fourth day of creation.

Then God said, "Let the waters be filled with living creatures and the skies be filled with birds." And they were. This was the fifth day of creation.

God then created animals to roam the earth. God looked down at His creation and saw that it was good. Finally, God created people. He made them in His very own image. God took dust from the ground and formed a man. And with His own breath, God breathed life into the man. He took a rib from the man and created a woman to be his helper and wife. They were called Adam and Eve.

God planted a garden in Eden, and He placed Adam and Eve in the garden to care for it. God said, "You may eat from any tree in the garden, but you must not eat from the tree of the knowledge of good and evil. If you eat from that tree, you will die." This all happened on the sixth day of creation.

On the seventh day of creation, God rested from all of His work.

**Christ Connection:** Colossians 1:15–22 reveals that Christ is ruler over all of God's creation. All of creation was created through Him, by Him, and for Him. Everything was created to give glory to Christ, but people would choose not to give Him glory. The rest of the Bible reveals how Jesus would restore the relationship between God and man.

**Big Picture Question:** Who created everything?

**Big Picture Answer:** God created everything. He created the world and people to bring Him glory.

In the garden of Eden, God gave Adam and Eve only one rule: do not eat the fruit from the tree of the knowledge of good and evil. If they ate it, they would die.

Now the serpent (who was really Satan) said to Eve, "Did God really say, 'You can't eat from any tree in the garden'?"

Eve said, "We may eat from any tree except the one in the middle of the garden. If we eat its fruit or even touch it, we will die."

"You won't die," lied the serpent. "You'll become like God, knowing good and evil."

So Eve ate the fruit and gave some to Adam. Suddenly, their eyes were opened, and they knew they were naked! They made themselves clothes from fig leaves. But when they heard God walking in the garden, they hid.

"Where are you?" God called.

Adam answered, "I was naked, so I hid."

"Who told you that you were naked?" God asked. "Did you eat the fruit I told you not to eat?"

Adam blamed Eve: "The woman gave it to me."

Eve blamed the serpent: "He lied to me."

Adam and Eve had disobeyed God, and God had to punish their sin. Eve would have great pain in childbirth, and Adam would have to work hard to get food from the ground. And one day, they would die. Then God drove them out of the garden.

Adam and Eve later had two sons named Cain and Abel. Abel was a shepherd, and Cain grew crops. One day, Cain gave God an offering of some of his crops, while Abel offered God the firstborn of his flock. God was pleased with Abel's offering, but not Cain's. Cain was very angry.

"Why are you angry?" God asked. "If you do what is right, you will be accepted too."

But Cain said to Abel, "Let's go to the fields." There, Cain attacked Abel and killed him!

"Where is Abel?" God asked Cain.

"I don't know," Cain lied.

But God knew what Cain had done, and He cursed him. "The ground will never again grow food for you, and you will wander the earth." Then God placed a mark on Cain so that no one would kill him. Cain left God's presence and went to the land of Nod, east of Eden.

Adam and Eve had other children, including a son named Seth.

**Christ Connection:** Adam and Eve failed to give God glory when they brought sin into the world, but God didn't leave them without hope. God sent His Son Jesus to live as Adam didn't—perfectly sinless. Jesus was God in the form of a man sent to rescue people from sin.

**Big Picture Question:** What is sin?

**Big Picture Answer:** Sin is breaking God's law, and it separates people from God.

# Noah and the Ark

One day, God looked at all the people on the earth and saw that their every thought was evil and full of sin. He was sorry that He had ever made man. So God said, "I will wipe man off the face of the earth."

But Noah was a good and righteous man who tried to follow God in all things. God wanted to save Noah, so He said to him, "Build an ark out of gopher wood. Make it 450 feet long, 75 feet wide, and 45 feet high." Then God told Noah exactly how to build the roof, where to put the door, and how to fix the rooms inside the ark.

God said, "I will flood the earth, and everything on it will die. But I will keep you safe. You will go into the ark with your sons, your wife, and your sons' wives. Take with you two of every living creature, male and female, to keep them alive too."

So Noah built the ark just as God told him. Then he, his family, and the animals went inside, and God shut the door. The rains came, and it rained for 40 days and 40 nights. The waters rose and covered the entire earth—even the mountains! Everything on dry land died. Only Noah and those in the ark lived. For 150 days, the water completely covered the earth.

Then God sent a wind to dry up the waters. After another 150 days, the ark landed on the mountains of Ararat (AIR uh rat). After 40 days, Noah opened the window and sent out a raven. The raven flew back and forth until the waters dried up. Then Noah sent out a dove, but she came back to the ark because she couldn't find a place to rest. After seven days, Noah sent the dove out again. This time she came back with an olive leaf. A week later, Noah sent the dove out again, and this time she didn't return. The ground was dry.

Noah, his family, and all the animals came out of the ark. God promised He would never again flood the whole earth. Then He placed a rainbow in the sky as a sign of His promise.

**Christ Connection:** The story of the flood shows us how serious God is about sin. He will not leave sin unpunished. But the story of Noah also shows us how loving God is. He provided a rescue plan for one righteous man—Noah. The rescue was extended to Noah's family. This story points ahead to a greater rescue! Jesus, the only perfectly righteous person, came to take the punishment for sin. We trust His act of obedience and are saved from the punishment our sin deserves.

**Big Picture Question:** Why does sin separate people from God?

**Big Picture Answer:** God is holy and separate from sin.

# The Tower of Babel

Genesis 9:1; 11:1–9

After Noah and his family left the ark, God blessed them. He told them to have many children and to fill the earth with people again. But the people found a valley in the land of Shinar (SHI nahr) and settled there. Now at that time, all the people spoke the same language.

The people began to say to one another, "Let's build ourselves a city and a tower with its top in the sky. We'll make a name for ourselves, and it will show how great we are. Then we won't have to be scattered over the whole earth." They were trying to bring glory to themselves instead of to God.

So the people began to make bricks, and they fired them in ovens until they were very hard. They used the bricks to build their city and its tower.

God came down to look at what the people were building. He said, "If they are doing this, they'll just keep thinking up more bad things to do. We need to stop them."

So God mixed up their languages and their words. When the people tried to make plans to build more of their city and tower, they couldn't understand each other! If one workman said, "Hand me another brick," nobody else knew what he wanted. Or if someone said, "Give me that hammer," he might be given a shovel instead! They had to stop building the city.

People began to move away in groups to live with those who spoke the same language. In this way, God scattered them over the face of the whole earth—which is what He had told the people to do after the flood.

The city with its unfinished tower was called Babel (BAY buhl), or Babylon (BAB uh luhn). It means "confused," because the people were confused when they tried to talk to one another.

**Christ Connection:** Instead of glorifying God, people chose to ignore God's plan and glorify themselves. This didn't stop God's plan to scatter the people and to form nations. Eventually one of these nations would become God's chosen people. Through the nation of Israel, Christ would come to save the world.

**Big Picture Question:** What happens when people sin?

**Big Picture Answer:** Sin separates people from God and one another.

Job was a great and godly man who followed God. He turned away from all evil and sin. Job was also very wealthy.

One day, God said to Satan, "Have you seen Job? No one else on the earth is like him. He turns away from all evil."

But Satan said, "That's because you bless and protect him. Take away everything Job has, and he will curse you."

"Very well," said God, "you may take away everything Job has, but do not hurt Job himself."

So Satan sent men to steal Job's oxen, donkeys, and camels. Then he sent lightning to kill his sheep. He even caused all 10 of Job's children to die! But Job still followed God.

So God said to Satan, "You've tried to turn Job against me, but it didn't work."

Satan said, "Take away Job's health, and he will curse you."

"Very well," said God, "but do not kill him."

So Job became sick. Painful boils covered his whole body. Job's wife told him to blame God, but Job would not. Job's friends told him that he was being punished for some terrible sin. But Job knew that he was innocent. He wished for a mediator—someone who would speak to God for him. Job even began to question why God had allowed all these things to happen to him.

Then God Himself spoke to Job from the whirlwind. "Where were you when I made the earth?" God asked. "Were you the one who told the sea where to stop? Did you command the morning to come? Or put the stars in their places? Do you know when the animals have their babies? Did you tell the eagle to fly?"

God asked all these questions and many more. God wanted Job to understand that He is all-powerful and ruler over all. Because Job was only a man, he could not fully understand God's ways.

Job said, "Surely I spoke about things I didn't understand, things too wonderful for me to know."

Then God gave Job 10 more children and twice as much wealth as he had before. Job lived 140 years after his suffering. He saw both his grandchildren and great-grandchildren before he died.

**Christ Connection:** Job's suffering and his request for a mediator give us a glimpse of our Savior, Jesus. Neither Job nor Jesus experienced suffering because they had sinned. Unlike Job, Jesus never questioned why He had to suffer. Jesus understood that we needed Him to pay the price for our sin and be our mediator before God.

**Big Picture Question:** Who is in control?

**Big Picture Answer:** God is all-powerful and in control.

Once there lived a man named Abram whose wife was named Sarai (SAR ay i). God told Abram to leave his home and go to a land that He would show him. He promised to make Abram's name great, and He said all the people on the earth would be blessed through him.

Abram obeyed God and left his home. Then God appeared to him in a vision and said, "Do not be afraid, Abram. I am your shield, and your reward will be very great."

Abram was sad, though. "What can You give me, God?" he asked. "I have no children, so one of my slaves will inherit everything I have." For both Abram and Sarai were too old to have children of their own.

But God had a plan. He took Abram outside and said, "Look at the sky and count the stars, if you can."

Of course, Abram couldn't count the stars. There were too many!

"Your offspring will be as many as the stars," God promised.

Abram believed God, and God was pleased. God also promised that Abram's family would keep the land they were living in.

"How can I be sure?" Abram asked.

So God gave Abram a sign that He would keep His covenant (or promise) with him. He told Abram to sacrifice a cow, a goat, a ram, a turtledove, and a pigeon. Abram did as God asked, and then fell into a deep sleep.

While he was sleeping, God told him what would happen in the future. He said Abram's family would be slaves in another country for 400 years before God would judge that nation and bless Abram's family. But Abram himself would live a long, peaceful life.

When the sun set and it was dark, a smoking fire pot and a flaming torch appeared. They passed between the animals as a sign that God would keep His promises.

**Christ Connection:** God chose Abram to be the father of the nation in which Jesus would be born. In this way, Abram would bless all nations, as God had promised. God also saw Abram's faith in God's promises and counted it as righteousness. It is faith in Jesus' perfect righteousness that brings salvation to God's people.

**Big Picture Question:** Why did God choose Abram?

**Big Picture Answer:** God chose Abram to be the father of the nation in which Jesus would be born.

# The Sons of Abraham

God promised Abram that he would have a child. But many years passed, and Abram and Sarai (SAR ay i) still had no child. So Sarai decided to fix the problem on her own.

"Since the Lord has kept me from having children," Sarai told Abram, "go to my slave. Perhaps I can build a family through her."

So Sarai gave her servant Hagar (HAY gahr) to Abram to be his wife. But when Hagar became pregnant, she began to look down on Sarai. Sarai complained to Abram, but he said, "Do whatever you want with her." Sarai treated Hagar so badly that she ran away.

The Angel of the Lord found Hagar by a spring of water in the wilderness. He said to her, "Hagar, where have you come from and where are you going?"

"I am running away from my mistress Sarai," Hagar answered.

"Go back to your mistress," the Angel of the Lord told her. "You will have a son. You will name him Ishmael (ISH may el) because the Lord has heard your cries." (Ishmael means "God hears.")

So Hagar went back to Sarai. She gave birth to Abram's son, and she named him Ishmael. Abram was 86 years old when Ishmael was born. But Ishmael was not the son of God's special promise to Abram.

Abram and Sarai waited 13 more years, then God appeared to Abram once again. He changed Abram's name to Abraham, which means "Father of a Great Multitude." This was because Abraham would be the father of many nations and kings.

God also changed Sarai's name to Sarah, which means "princess." God said, "I will bless her, and I will give you a son by her. She will be the mother of nations and kings."

Abraham laughed to himself, "How can a child be born to 100-year-old man and a woman who is 90?"

But God said, "In one year, Sarah will have a son, and you will name him Isaac. I will make My covenant with him and his future offspring. I will bless Ishmael, too, and he will be a great nation. But My covenant will be with Isaac."

God kept His promise. A year later, Sarah gave birth to a son. Abraham named his son Isaac, just as God had told him to do. Abraham was 100 years old when Isaac was born. He had learned that God always keeps His promises.

**Christ Connection:** God fulfilled His promise to Abraham by giving him a son. Isaac was the hope of Abraham and Sarah for a future and a legacy. God fulfilled His promise to the world by giving us His Son. Jesus ultimately fulfilled God's promise to Abraham, and He is the hope of the world for salvation and redemption.

**Big Picture Question:** Who always keeps His promises?

**Big Picture Answer:** God always keeps His promises. We can trust in Him.

God kept His promise to give Abraham a son, but God wanted to make sure He was still the most important thing in Abraham's life. So He tested Abraham to see if he would obey Him.

"Abraham," God called.

"Here I am," answered Abraham.

"Take your son Isaac, whom you love, and go to the land of Moriah," God said. "Take him up to the mountain and offer him as a sacrifice."

Now a sacrifice is something of great value that is given to God. It can be obedience, love, thanksgiving, or the need for forgiveness. In Old Testament times, a sacrifice was usually an animal that was killed on an altar. This time, though, God asked Abraham to sacrifice his son Isaac on the altar instead.

With a heavy heart, Abraham got up early the next morning. He gathered some wood, and he saddled his donkey. Then he set out with his son Isaac and two servants. They traveled for three days to reach the place God told him about. Abraham then left his servants with the donkey, while he and Isaac went a little farther up the mountain. Isaac carried the wood, and Abraham carried the knife and the fire.

Isaac saw that something was missing. "Father," he asked, "where is the lamb for the sacrifice?"

"God Himself will give us the lamb," Abraham answered.

When they got to the place God had told him about, Abraham built an altar and placed the wood on top. He tied up his son Isaac and placed him on top of the altar. Then Abraham took the knife and was about to sacrifice his son.

But the Angel of the Lord called to him from heaven, "Abraham, Abraham! Do not hurt the boy. Now I know that you fear God. You were willing to give up your only son for Me."

Abraham then looked up and saw a ram trapped by its horns in the bushes. He offered the ram to God, and he named that place, "The Lord Will Provide."

The Angel of the Lord spoke to Abraham again. "I will bless you," He said. "I will make your family as many as the stars of the sky and the sand on the seashore. Your enemies will be defeated. All nations of the earth will be blessed because you have obeyed Me."

**Christ Connection:** Abraham showed his faith in God when he was willing to sacrifice Isaac. Isaac also showed he was ready to do what his father said. This was a clear picture of God who was willing to sacrifice His only Son, and of Jesus who was willing to do what was necessary for God's plan of salvation. Isaac's life was spared because God provided a substitute. We need a perfect sacrifice as our substitute for sin. God provided a perfect sacrifice in His Son, Jesus Christ.

**Big Picture Question:** How can we show we believe God's plan?

**Big Picture Answer:** We obey God even when He asks us to do things we don't understand.

# God Remembered His Promise

God had promised Abraham that his offspring would be like the stars in the sky and the sand on the seashore—too many to be counted! But Abraham's son Isaac had no children. For 20 years, Isaac prayed that God would give his wife, Rebekah, a child.

At last, God answered Isaac's prayers—Rebekah was going to have twins! But the two babies fought inside her. This worried Rebekah, so she went to God and asked, "Why is this happening?"

God told her, "The babies in your womb will become two nations. One people will be stronger than the other, and the older will serve the younger."

When the babies were born, they were both boys. The first baby was red-looking and covered with hair. They named him Esau (EE saw). The younger baby was born holding on to Esau's heel. They named him Jacob.

Years later, there was a famine in the land. In Egypt, there was food, but God appeared to Isaac and said, "Don't go to Egypt. Stay in this land. I will give all these lands to you and your offspring, just as I promised Abraham." So Isaac obeyed God.

Years after that, God appeared again. This time it was to Isaac's son Jacob. Jacob had betrayed his brother Esau and lied to his father. He had fled his home so that Esau wouldn't kill him. As he traveled, Jacob stopped one night to sleep. He took a stone and put it under his head for a pillow.

While Jacob slept, he dreamed of a stairway that reached from the ground all the way up to heaven! God's angels were going up and down it. Then God spoke to Jacob and said, "I am the God of Abraham and Isaac. I will give you and your offspring the land you are sleeping on. Your offspring will be like the dust of the earth. All people will be blessed through you and your offspring. I am with you. I will watch over you wherever you go. And I will bring you back to this land."

Jacob took the stone he had used as a pillow and poured oil over it. Then he named that place Bethel, which means "House of God."

**Christ Connection:** God's wonderful plan to Abraham extended well beyond his lifetime. The plan was shared with Rebekah, Isaac, Jacob, and eventually an entire nation leading to the birth of a baby boy named Jesus. Jesus fulfilled God's plan to provide salvation and redemption for all of God's people.

**Big Picture Question:** How did people know God's plan?

**Big Picture Answer:** God told people His plan.

# The Stolen Blessing

Jacob and Esau grew into young men. Esau became a hunter, while Jacob worked at home. Their father, Isaac, loved Esau best. But their mother, Rebekah, loved Jacob.

One day, when Jacob was cooking a stew, Esau came in from the field. "I'm so tired. Give me some of that stew," said Esau.

"First, sell me your birthright," Jacob said. (The birthright belonged to the oldest child. It gave him more of his family's wealth when his parents died.)

"I'm going to die from hunger! What good is a birthright to me?" Esau said. So he sold his birthright to Jacob for a bowl of stew, because he did not think it was important.

Later, when Isaac was an old man, his eyes became so weak that he could not see. He said to Esau, "I am old, and I don't know when I will die. Hunt some game for me, and make me my favorite meal. Then I will bless you." (This blessing would make Esau the family's leader.)

Rebekah heard this. So when Esau left, she said to Jacob, "Bring me two young goats. I will make them into your father's favorite meal. Take it to him, and he'll bless you instead."

But Jacob said, "Esau is hairy, and I have smooth skin. What if my father touches me? He'll know I'm a liar, and he'll curse me."

Rebekah said, "The curse will be on me. Just do what I say."

So Jacob brought the goats to her, and she cooked them. She put the goat skins on his hands and neck to make him hairy. Then Jacob took the food to his father.

"I am Esau," Jacob said. "Please eat so that you may bless me."

"Come closer," Isaac said, and he touched the goat skins on Jacob's hands. Then he said, "The voice is Jacob's, but the hands are Esau's. Are you really Esau?"

"I am," Jacob lied.

So Isaac ate the meal and blessed Jacob. The blessing included land, riches, and power. "May nations bow down to you," Isaac said. "Be master over your brothers."

Soon after, Esau returned and brought his father his favorite meal. Then Isaac knew he had been tricked! Esau begged his father to bless him, too, but it was too late.

Esau was so angry! He decided to kill Jacob when Isaac died. Rebekah heard this and sent Jacob away to live with her brother.

**Christ Connection:** Jacob is a perfect example of why a Savior was needed. Like Jacob, we seek a birthright and blessing that is not ours, but we cannot lie, deceive, or trick to receive it. Instead Jesus shared His birthright and blessing with us when He paid for our sins on the cross and gave us His righteousness.

**Big Picture Question:** What can stop God's plans?

**Big Picture Answer:** Nothing can stop God's plans because they are always perfect.

# Jacob's New Name

Jacob lived away from his home for many years. He had wives and children and flocks of his own. Then one day, God said, "Go back to the land of your fathers and to your family. I will be with you."

So Jacob put his children and wives on camels. He gathered his herds and began the journey home. Going home meant that Jacob would see his brother Esau again. Jacob worried that Esau might still be angry with him for stealing his blessing. So he sent messengers ahead to tell Esau that Jacob, his servant, was coming.

When the messengers returned, they said to Jacob, "Your brother is coming to meet you—and he has 400 men with him!"

Jacob was afraid, so he split his family and servants into two groups. He hoped that if Esau attacked one group, the others could escape. Jacob then asked to God to protect him and to keep His promise that his family would be like the sand of the seashore—too many to count. Jacob also sent ahead of him large gifts of goats, sheep, camels, cows, bulls, and donkeys.

Later that night, Jacob moved his family across the stream, while he stayed alone on the other side. A man—who was actually God—came and wrestled with him all night. Then He said to Jacob, "Let Me go, for it is daybreak."

But Jacob said, "I will not let You go unless You bless me."

So the man said, "Your name will no longer be Jacob. It will be Israel because you have struggled with God." Then He blessed him.

Jacob named that place "Peniel" (PEHN ih ehl), which means "face of God." This was because he had seen God face to face. After this, Jacob looked up. He saw Esau and his 400 men coming toward him. Jacob went to meet Esau, bowing as he got near his brother. But Esau ran to meet Jacob, threw his arms around him, and kissed him. They wept together.

"Why did you send all these gifts ahead of you?" Esau asked.

"To please you, my lord," Jacob said.

"I have enough, my brother," Esau told him. "Keep what you have."

But Jacob said, "Please take these, because God has been good to me, and I have everything I need." Then Jacob settled with all this family at Shechem (SHEE kem).

**Christ Connection:** Jacob's meeting with God changed his life as reflected in his new name, Israel. Jesus came so that we might have a changed life, forgiven of sin (2 Corinthians 5:17). Jesus' death and resurrection provided sinful people with the way to be adopted into God's family. When we are adopted into the family of God we also receive a new name—children of God (John 1:12).

**Big Picture Question:** What new name did God give Jacob?

**Big Picture Answer:** God changed Jacob's name to Israel, which became the name of God's chosen people.

# Joseph Sent to Egypt

Jacob had 12 sons, but Joseph was his favorite. Jacob even gave Joseph a special robe of many colors. When Joseph's brothers saw this, they hated him.

One day, Joseph had a dream: "I dreamed we were gathering bundles of grain. Suddenly, my bundle stood up, while yours bowed down to it." This made Joseph's brothers hate him even more. Then he had another dream. In it, the sun, moon, and 11 stars bowed to Joseph. Even Jacob scolded Joseph this time. "Will your mother, brothers, and I all bow to you?" he said.

A little later, Jacob sent Joseph to check on his brothers, who were out tending their flocks. The brothers saw him coming and decided to kill him. But Reuben, the oldest, told them to throw him into a pit instead. He planned to rescue Joseph later.

The brothers grabbed Joseph, tore off his colorful robe, and threw him into the pit. While they were eating, they saw a caravan of Ishmaelites (ISH mayehl aits) heading to Egypt. They sold Joseph to them as a slave. Then they dipped his robe in goat's blood and told Jacob that a wild animal had killed his son. Jacob was sad for a long time.

Joseph was sold to an Egyptian officer named Potiphar. God was with Joseph, though, and gave him success at everything he did. So Potiphar put Joseph in charge of his household. But then Potiphar's wife told a terrible lie about Joseph, and he was thrown in jail!

Even in jail, God blessed Joseph. He was put in charge of all the prisoners. At that time, Pharaoh's cupbearer and baker were also in jail. They told Joseph about their dreams. With God's help, Joseph told them what the dreams meant: the cupbearer would serve Pharaoh again, but the baker would be killed. "Remember me to Pharaoh," Joseph told the cupbearer, but he forgot.

Two years later, Pharaoh dreamed that seven fat cows were eaten by seven skinny cows. Then, seven fat heads of grain were eaten by seven thin heads. No one could tell Pharaoh the meaning of his dreams. Then the cupbearer remembered Joseph!

Joseph was brought to Pharaoh. With God's help, Joseph explained what the dreams meant. There would be seven years with plenty of food, then seven years of famine with no food. Pharaoh saw that God was with Joseph, so he put him in charge of all Egypt. Joseph was second only to Pharaoh.

**Christ Connection:** God sent Joseph to Egypt and blessed him, so that he rose to a position of great power. In that position, he was God's instrument for saving his family and many others in the world from death by starvation. Jesus gave up his position of great power to be God's instrument for saving people. Christ's life and death made a way to save people from spiritual death, which is the penalty of sin.

**Big Picture Question:** Who is always with us?

**Big Picture Answer:** God is always with us, even when things happen that we don't understand.

The famine came, just as God had said. It was not only in Egypt, but in every land. Joseph had stored up grain during the seven good years, so there was food in Egypt. Every nation came to Joseph to buy grain. Even Jacob sent 10 of his sons to buy grain, but Benjamin—his youngest son—stayed home.

Joseph's brothers came and bowed down before him. He knew instantly who they were, but they didn't know him. As they bowed, Joseph remembered his dreams from long ago. Then he said, "You are spies!" and he threw them in jail for three days.

On the third day, Joseph said, "Prove to me that you aren't spies by bringing your youngest brother here." Then he kept one brother in prison and sent the other nine home.

When the brothers got home, they told Jacob everything, but he would not let them take Benjamin to Egypt. The famine was terrible, though. When they had used up all the grain, Jacob sent them back to Egypt to buy more—and he let Benjamin go with them.

When Joseph saw Benjamin with his brothers, he invited them to his house for lunch. Joseph gave Benjamin five times more food than his brothers.

After eating, Joseph told a servant to fill each man's bag with grain. He also told the servant to hide one of his silver cups in Benjamin's sack. After the brothers left, Joseph sent his servant after them to accuse them of stealing the cup.

The brothers said, "We didn't steal your master's cup. If any of us has it, he will die and the rest of us will be your slaves."

When the cup was found in Benjamin's sack, the brothers were very afraid. They returned to Joseph's house. Joseph told them they could leave, but Benjamin would be kept as his slave. His brother Judah begged to take Benjamin's place.

Joseph was overcome by his feelings that he couldn't hide who he was any longer. He sent his servants away, and told them he was their brother. The brothers were terrified, but Joseph said, "Don't be afraid. You planned evil against me, but God used it to bring about great good."

Then Joseph said, "Go home and get my father and all your families. Bring them here. You can settle in the land of Goshen and be near me."

This is how the Israelites came to live in Egypt.

**Christ Connection:** Joseph recognized that though his brothers intended evil, God planned his circumstances for good—to establish a remnant of God's people (Genesis 45:7). Likewise, though those who crucified Jesus intended it for evil, God's plan for the sacrifice of His Son was for the good of all people. Through Jesus' death on the cross, God again saved a remnant of people.

**Big Picture Question:** Why did God send Joseph to Egypt?

**Big Picture Answer:** God sent Joseph to Egypt to save his family—and God's chosen people, the Israelites.

Many years passed, and Joseph died. A new pharaoh came to power. He didn't know about the wonderful things Joseph had done for Egypt. This Pharaoh was afraid of the Israelites (also called Hebrews), because there were so many of them. So he made them his slaves. But the harder the Israelites worked, the bigger their families grew.

So Pharaoh gave this order, "Throw every Hebrew baby boy into the Nile River!"

Now, there was a woman who gave birth to a baby boy. For 3 months, she hid him. When she could no longer hide him, she put him in a basket in the reeds by the Nile River. The baby's older sister, Miriam, hid and watched over the basket.

When Pharaoh's daughter went down to the river to bathe, she found the baby and felt sorry for him. "This is one of the Hebrew boys," she said, and she named him Moses.

Miriam stepped out and said, "Should I get a Hebrew woman to care for him?"

"Go," said Pharaoh's daughter, and Miriam ran to get her mother.

Moses grew up in Pharaoh's palace, but he saw how badly his people were treated. One day, Moses killed an Egyptian for beating a Hebrew slave. Pharaoh found out and tried to kill Moses. He ran away to Midian (MID ih uhn) and stayed there many years, working as a shepherd. But the Israelites were still suffering, and they cried out to God. He heard their cries, and He had a plan to save them.

One day, as Moses was watching over his flock, he saw something strange. A bush was on fire, but it was not being burned up! God called to him from the bush, "Moses!"

"Here I am," Moses answered.

God said, "I have seen how My people are suffering. Go back to Pharaoh and lead My people out of Egypt."

But Moses said, "What if they don't believe You sent me?"

So God gave Moses three miracles to perform. He turned Moses' staff into a snake and his hand white with leprosy. Finally, He told Moses that if he poured water from the Nile River onto the ground, it would turn into blood.

"But I'm not good at speaking!" Moses said. "Send someone else."

God was angry because Moses didn't trust Him. But He sent Moses' brother, Aaron, to help him. Finally, Moses went to Egypt.

**Christ Connection:** God saved Moses for a special purpose: to rescue His people. The calling of Moses points to a greater calling and rescue—the call of Jesus to come to earth to save God's people from their sin. Moses and Jesus both obeyed God's commands in order to carry out His plan of salvation. Moses delivered God's people from physical captivity; Jesus delivered God's people from captivity to sin.

**Big Picture Question:** Why did God save Moses?

**Big Picture Answer:** God saved Moses to rescue His people from captivity.

# Moses Confronted Pharaoh

After God called Moses to lead His people out of Egypt, Moses and Aaron went to Pharaoh. They said, "This is what Yahweh the God of Israel says: Let My people go, so that they may worship Me in the wilderness."

But Pharaoh said, "Who is this Yahweh? Why should I obey Him? I will not let Israel go!" Pharaoh was angry. He thought Moses was trying to stop the people from working hard, so he ordered them to work even harder.

When the Israelites heard this, they were angry. "You're making trouble for us!" they told Moses.

Moses asked God, "Why have You caused trouble for this people?"

But God said, "I will deliver you from Egypt. Pharaoh's heart is hard. He will not listen, but I will stretch out My hand against Egypt. The Egyptians will know that I am Yahweh." Then God sent 10 plagues to punish Pharaoh and the Egyptian people.

First, God turned the Nile River to blood. All the fish died, and people could not drink from it. Still, Pharaoh would not let the Israelites go.

Then, God sent frogs into Egypt. They covered the land and even filled the beds, ovens, and bowls! Pharaoh called for Moses, "Ask your God to take the frogs away. Then I will let your people go." But when the frogs were gone, Pharaoh refused to let the people go.

Next, God filled the land with gnats. After that, He sent flies. They swarmed all over Egypt, but there were none where the Israelites lived. Then, God made all the livestock die—all the horses, donkeys, camels, and sheep. All the animals in Egypt died, but none of the Israelites' animals died. Still, Pharaoh would not let the people go.

So God sent painful boils to cover all the people in Egypt. Then came a terrible hailstorm that smashed every plant and every tree. After that, God sent clouds of locusts that ate up every living plant. But there were no boils or storms or locusts where the Israelites lived.

For the ninth plague, God sent three days of darkness to cover Egypt. Only the Israelites had light. After all this, Pharaoh still would not let the Israelites go!

Then God said to Moses, "I will bring one more plague—the most terrible one of all. After that, Pharaoh will let you go."

**Christ Connection:** God called Moses to be His servant. He was a great servant who obeyed God and led the Israelites out of slavery. The Bible says that Jesus is greater than Moses (Hebrews 3:3). Jesus was a servant who obeyed God perfectly and suffered to free His people from sin.

**Big Picture Question:** What did God show the Egyptians and the Israelites?

**Big Picture Answer:** God showed that He is the one true God.

There had been 9 terrible plagues in Egypt, but Pharaoh's heart was still hard. He would not let the Israelites go.

So God said to Moses, "I will bring one more plague on Pharaoh and on Egypt. After that, he will let you go."

Moses went to Pharaoh and told him exactly what would happen: "About midnight, God will go through Egypt, and every firstborn male in the land will die—from Pharaoh's firstborn to the firstborn of the servant girl. Even the firstborn of the livestock will die. There will be a great cry of sadness throughout Egypt, but none of the Israelites will be harmed. Then you and your officials will bow before me and tell us to leave."

Still, Pharaoh would not listen.

God told Moses what the Israelites must do to be saved that night. Every family must choose a lamb or goat, without any spot or blemish. It must be killed and its blood sprinkled on the doorposts of the house. This would be a sign for God to "pass over" that house, so that no one in that family would die.

God also told the Israelites to roast the meat with bitter herbs and to bake unleavened bread (bread without yeast). They were to eat this meal at midnight. "Eat with your sandals on and be dressed to travel," God said. "Eat in a hurry and be ready to go!"

The Israelites did just as God said. That night, while the Egyptians were sleeping, the Israelites were busy making their meal and putting blood on their doorposts.

At midnight, God struck every firstborn in the land of Egypt. Pharaoh's son died. The prisoner's son died. The firstborn of the livestock died. Every house in Egypt had someone die.

Pharaoh called for Moses and Aaron during the night. "Get up! Leave my people, and go!" he ordered. "Take your flocks and herds, and leave!"

The Israelites quickly gathered their things. As they left, God gave them favor in the Egyptians' eyes, and they gave the Israelites silver and gold and clothing. Then a whole army of Israelites—600,000 men and their families—left Egypt.

God lead His people out of Egypt. He was preparing a place for them in the land of Canaan (KAY nuhn). For 430 years, the Israelites had been slaves in the land of Egypt. They were finally free!

**Christ Connection:** By His grace, God spared the Israelites from judgment by requiring the blood of a lamb. Jesus is the Lamb of God, who takes away the sin of the world. His death was the ultimate sacrifice, and those who trust in Christ are under His saving blood and will be passed over in the final judgment.

**Big Picture Question:** Why is the Passover important?

**Big Picture Answer:** The Passover was the way God chose to save His people. It's a picture of the sacrifice Jesus would one day make for sinners.

# The Israelites Crossed the Red Sea

After the tenth plague, the Israelites quickly left Egypt. The Lord led them toward the Red Sea. During the day, He led them in a pillar of cloud. At night, He led them in a pillar of fire to give them light. God told Moses to have the people camp near the sea.

When Pharaoh was told that the Israelites really had left Egypt, he changed his mind. "What have we done?" he said. "We've lost our slaves!" Pharaoh gathered his army and more than 600 chariots. Then he got into his own chariot, and they chased after the Israelites. They caught up with them near the Red Sea.

The Israelites saw the Egyptians coming. "We're going to die!" they cried. "We never should have left Egypt!"

But Moses said, "Don't be afraid. The Lord will fight for you, and you'll never see these Egyptians again."

God said to Moses: "Lift up your staff. Stretch out your hand over the sea. Part it so that the Israelites can walk across on dry ground." Then the pillar of cloud moved behind the Israelites to hold back the Egyptians for the night.

Moses stretched out his hand, and the Lord parted the sea. The Israelites walked through the sea on dry ground! A wall of water rose up on each side of them.

The Egyptians chased after them into the sea. But as soon as the Israelites were safely across, Moses stretched out his hand again. The waters came crashing back and covered the entire Egyptian army. Not one of them lived.

Then Moses and the Israelites sang a song of praise to God:

*The Lord is my strength and my song.*
*He has become my salvation.*

Moses led the people away from the Red Sea and into the wilderness. But they began to grumble because they couldn't find water to drink. Moses cried out to God, and He gave them water.

Later, the Israelites became hungry. Again they grumbled, saying, "We were better off living in Egypt! You brought us out here to die!"

God said, "At twilight, I will give you meat. In the morning, I will rain bread from heaven."

So at evening, quail came into the camp. And in the morning, fine flakes of bread were on the ground like a frost. The Israelites called it manna, which means, "What is it?" In this way, God took care of His people.

**Christ Connection:** God created a way for the Israelites to escape the Egyptians. In the same way, God created the way for people to escape the penalty of sin—His Son, Jesus Christ. Jesus is the only way to get to God.

**Big Picture Question:** Is anything too hard for God to do?

**Big Picture Answer:** Nothing is impossible for God.

Three months after the Israelites left Egypt, they came into the Wilderness of Sinai (SIGH nigh). They camped in front of the mountain. Moses went up the mountain to God, and God said to him, "Tell the Israelites: If you listen to Me and keep My covenant, you will be My people."

Moses went back to the people and told them what God had said. "We will do all that the Lord says," they told him.

Then God said to Moses, "I will come to you in a dense cloud. I want the people to hear Me speak to you, so that they'll believe you."

Moses got the people ready. On the third day, thunder and lightning rumbled. A thick cloud came down upon the mountain, and a loud trumpet sounded. The people shuddered. Then Moses brought them to the foot of the mountain. The mountain shook, and the trumpet got louder. Moses spoke, and God answered him in the thunder.

Then God told Moses to come to the top of the mountain. There, He gave Moses the Ten Commandments:

Do not have other gods besides Me.

Do not make an idol for yourself.

Do not misuse the name of the Lord your God.

Remember the Sabbath day, to keep it holy.

Honor your father and your mother.

Do not murder.

Do not commit adultery.

Do not steal.

Do not give false testimony about your neighbor.

Do not covet your neighbor's possessions.

When God finished speaking, He gave Moses 2 stone tablets that He had written on with His own finger.

Moses was on the mountain for 40 days. He was gone so long that the Israelites went to Aaron and said, "Make a god to lead us because we don't know where Moses is." So Aaron made a golden calf for them to worship.

God saw this and was very angry. Moses hurried down the mountain, carrying the two stone tablets. When Moses saw the people dancing before the golden calf, he was so angry that he threw down the stone tablets, smashing them to pieces. Moses destroyed the golden calf, then he went back to God. "Please forgive them," Moses begged.

But God punished the people with a plague because they had worshipped the golden calf. Then God made Moses 2 more stone tablets to replace the ones he had broken.

**Christ Connection:** God made a covenant with His people: "If you obey Me, you will be My people" (Exodus 19:5–6). But the people did not obey God. They sinned against God, and Moses asked God to forgive them. Moses acted as their mediator, or advocate, before God. When we sin, Jesus is our mediator. Through Jesus, we are forgiven of our sins. God is pleased with us because He looks at Jesus, who never sinned.

**Big Picture Question:** Why did God give His people the Ten Commandments?

**Big Picture Answer:** God is holy. He gave them laws to help them be holy too.

# The Tabernacle Was Built

When Moses was on the mountain talking to God, God said, "Tell the Israelites to make a place for Me—a tabernacle—so that I may live among them. Make it exactly as I tell you."

Moses told the Israelites what God had said. He asked them to bring gifts to God for the tabernacle—gold, silver, and bronze; yarns, fine linen, and goat hair; animal skins; wood; oil; spices; and gemstones.

The Israelites began bringing their gifts. God gave two men—Bezalel (BEHZ uh lehl) and Oholiab (oh HOH lih ab)—the ability to do every kind of craft and creative work. Then they taught others, and so all the skilled people came together to build the tabernacle. All this time, the people kept bringing gifts. Soon, the craftsmen came to Moses and said, "The people are bringing more than we need to build the tabernacle." So Moses told the Israelites to stop bringing gifts.

The tabernacle was made just as God had said. Curtains of linen formed the walls. Over them hung curtains of goat hair, which formed a tent over the tabernacle. Many things were made for the inside of the tabernacle: lampstands, tables, bowls, utensils, and the ark of the covenant. (The ark was a wooden box covered in gold. It represented God's presence among the people.) Special robes and garments were made for the priests. Every piece of the tabernacle had its own special purpose and was made just as God had said.

When everything was finished, God told Moses how to set up the tabernacle and where to put each thing inside it. God also told him how to anoint the tabernacle with oil so that it would be holy. Next, God told Moses to bring Aaron and his sons to the entrance of the tabernacle. They were to be His priests. Aaron put on the holy robes, and Moses anointed him as priest. Aaron's sons were also anointed.

When all was finished, the cloud covered the tabernacle, and God's glory filled it. Then God gave this sign to the people: If the cloud covered the tabernacle, the Israelites would stay where they were. When the cloud lifted, they would move on and take the tabernacle with them. The cloud of the Lord was over the tabernacle during the day, and there was a fire inside the cloud at night. So the Israelites could always see the cloud of God.

**Christ Connection:** God instructed the Israelites to build a tabernacle so that He could dwell with them. God desires to be with His people. As part of His plan of salvation, God sent Jesus to "tabernacle," or dwell with people on the earth.

**Big Picture Question:** What does the tabernacle show about God?

**Big Picture Answer:** God wants to dwell with His people and be worshipped by them.

# God Gave Rules for Sacrifice

When Moses was with God on Mount Sinai, God gave him many rules and laws for the Israelites to obey. Because God is holy, He said the people must obey His laws perfectly. To break a law is to sin, and God cannot be around sin. That's why He wants His people to be holy.

When the tabernacle was finished, Moses no longer had to go up the mountain to meet with God. He could go into the tabernacle. From there, God gave Moses more laws. These laws told the Israelites how to worship God and how to live holy lives.

First, God gave rules about offerings. Offerings are gifts people give to God, such as money or jewelry. Offerings could also be grain or bread or animals. Different offerings were needed at different times. When people wanted to praise God, they gave burnt offerings. When they wanted to say they were sorry for sin, they gave a sin offering.

God also gave rules about the priests. These rules told the priests how they should offer sacrifices, take care of the tabernacle, and teach the people about God's rules for living holy lives. Aaron and his sons were the first priests.

God told Moses about a special day that would happen once a year. It was called the Day of Atonement. Atonement means to make right the things that are wrong. The people needed to atone for their sins. They needed to make their relationship with God right again.

On the Day of Atonement, the high priest would offer a special sacrifice. He would take the blood of an animal and go into the most holy place in the tabernacle. There, he would sprinkle the blood on the mercy seat of the ark of the covenant (This was sometimes called the ark of God. Inside it were the stone tablets on which the Ten Commandments were written.) God said, "On that day your sins will be paid for. You will be made pure and clean. You will be clean from all of your sins in My sight."

God also gave the Israelites rules about how they should live. He said, "Be holy because I am holy." Then God told the people how to be holy: "Do not tell lies. Do not cheat. Love your neighbor as you love yourself. Obey My rules."

**Christ Connection:** The book of Leviticus contains many rules for the Israelites, but we do not obey all the rules in Leviticus today because we trust Jesus, who obeyed the law perfectly for us. The Israelites had to make a blood sacrifice for their sin every year. Jesus sacrificed His blood on the cross to pay for our sin once and for all (Hebrews 7:26–27). When we trust in Christ, God forgives us of our sin.

**Big Picture Question:** Why did God give rules for sacrifice?

**Big Picture Answer:** God gave rules to show how to worship Him and be forgiven for sin.

When the Israelites reached the edge of the promised land, God told Moses, "Send 12 men to scout out the land of Canaan (KAY nuhn). This is the land I am giving to the Israelites. Send one man from each family tribe."

Moses gathered the men just as God said. "Go and see what the land is like," Moses told them. "Are the people there strong or weak? Are there few or many? Is the land good?"

"Be courageous," Moses said as the spies left. "And bring back some fruit from the land."

For 40 days, the spies traveled all throughout the land. They cut down a cluster of grapes that was so big it had to be carried on a pole by two men! They also gathered pomegranates and figs. Then they went back to Moses and the Israelites.

"The land is flowing with milk and honey, and here is some of its fruit," they said. "But the people living there are strong, and the cities are large and fortified."

Caleb, one of the 12 spies, said, "We can take the land with God's help! We must take it!"

But the other men said, "No! We can't go up against those people. They're stronger than we are! We looked like grasshoppers next to them!"

The Israelites started to weep, and they wept all night. They thought Moses and Aaron had brought them to Canaan to die. "Let's get a new leader and go back to Egypt!" they said.

Moses and Aaron fell on their faces before the Israelites. Joshua and Caleb (who was also one of the spies) tore their clothes and said, "The land is very good. The Lord will give it to us. Don't be afraid of the people living there. God is with us!"

But God was angry. "How long will these people not trust Me?" he said to Moses.

God wanted to destroy all the Israelites, but Moses said, "Please forgive them, because You are great and faithful and loving."

So God said, "I'll forgive them, but none of them will live to see the promised land!"

The Israelites would have to wander in the wilderness for 40 years—one year for each day the spies spent in the promised land. Only Caleb and Joshua, who had trusted God completely, would be allowed to enter the promised land.

**Christ Connection:** Even though Joshua was not perfect, he lived a life of obedience to God. Joshua was faithful and was going to lead the people into the promised land. His accomplishments point to Christ's finished work on the cross—defeating Satan, setting people free from sin, and making the way into the promised land of eternity.

**Big Picture Question:** What happens when God's people sin?

**Big Picture Answer:** Sin has to be punished, but God promises to forgive when people seek forgiveness.

# The Bronze Snake Numbers 16:1–3; 17:1–12; 20:1–12, 14–20; 21:4–9

The Israelites had not trusted God, so He did not allow them to go into the promised land. Instead, they had to wander in the wilderness for 40 years. Along the way, the Israelites grumbled and complained.

First, they whined: "Why should Moses and Aaron be over us? We don't need them to tell us what to do."

So God told Moses to gather a staff from each of the 12 tribes and bring them to the tabernacle. God said: "The staff of the man I choose for my priest will sprout. That will stop the Israelites from complaining about you."

Moses gathered the staffs and placed them in front of the tabernacle. The next morning, Aaron's staff had not only sprouted, but it had also grown flowers and almonds! God showed the people that Aaron was His chosen priest.

Next, the people complained because they didn't have water to drink. God told Moses and Aaron to stand in front of the people and speak to a rock, then water would come out of the rock. But Moses was so angered by the people's grumbling that he hit the rock with his staff two times. The water came out, but Moses had disobeyed God. Because of that, Moses would not be allowed to go into the promised land.

Soon after, the Israelites were going to travel through the land of Edom (EE duhm), but the people of Edom wouldn't let them. The Israelites had to travel around it. It was a long, hard journey, and the Israelites began to grumble: "Why have you led us out of Egypt to die?"

God was so angry with His people that He sent poisonous snakes among them. The snakes bit many of them and they died. The people knew they had sinned by grumbling against God. So they begged Moses, "Please ask God to take the snakes away."

Moses spoke to God, and He said, "Make a snake image and put it on a pole. When anyone who is bitten looks at it, he will be healed."

So Moses made a bronze snake and put it on a pole. Those who were bitten, looked up at the bronze snake and were healed.

The Israelites had sinned against God, but He still loved them. He punished their sin, but He also gave them a way to be healed.

**Christ Connection:** The Israelites faced a huge problem because of their sin. God sent snakes to punish them. Anyone who was bitten could look at the snake on the pole and not die. Because of our sin, we face a huge problem: we are separated from God. We deserve to die. Anyone who looks to Jesus on the cross and trusts in Him will be saved and be made right with God.

**Big Picture Question:** What happens when people tell God they are sorry for their sins?

**Big Picture Answer:** God forgives them and gives them a way to be healed—through Jesus.

# Balaam and the Donkey

The Israelites had wandered in the wilderness for 40 years. At last, they were once again at the edge of the promised land. They camped in the plains of Moab (MOH ab), near the Jordan River. Now King Balak (BAY lak) of Moab was afraid of the Israelites. They might attack Moab!

So Balak sent messengers to Balaam (BAY luhm), a false prophet. "Come and curse the Israelites," he said. For he knew that those Balaam cursed were cursed, and those he blessed were blessed.

Balaam said to the messengers, "Spend the night here, and I will give you the Lord's answer."

Even though Balaam was not a follower of God, the Lord spoke to him and said, "Don't go with these men. Don't curse the Israelites because they are blessed."

Balaam told the men what God had said, and they went back to the king. But the king sent more messengers, begging Balaam to curse the Israelites.

This time God said, "Go with these men, but only do what I tell you."

Balaam saddled his donkey and left, but God sent an angel to stop him. Balaam couldn't see the angel, but his donkey could. Three times the angel stood in the way, and three times the donkey stopped. Each time, Balaam became angry and hit her.

Suddenly, God made the donkey talk! "Why have you hit me?" the donkey asked.

Balaam was so angry, he didn't even stop to wonder why his donkey was talking! "You made me look like a fool!" Balaam said.

Then God let Balaam see the angel. "I have sinned!" Balaam cried. "I'll go back if you want me to."

The angel said, "No, go with these men. But only say what I tell you."

When Balaam arrived, the king took him to where the Israelites were camping. Balaam went to a nearby hill and spoke to God. When he returned, Balaam blessed the Israelites as God told him. The king was not happy! But Balaam said, "I can only say what God tells me."

Twice more, the king took Balaam to look out over the Israelite's camp. And twice more, Balaam blessed them. "Enough!" the king said. "Go home!"

But Balaam had one more message: "A star will come from Jacob, and a scepter will arise from Israel." He was speaking about Jesus, who would one day come and defeat Israel's enemies. Then Balaam went home.

**Christ Connection:** Fourteen hundred years after Balaam announced Jesus' birth, wise men followed a star to the place where Jesus was born. The wise men worshiped Jesus as King (Matthew 2:2).

**Big Picture Question:** Who protected God's people?

**Big Picture Answer:** God protected His people from their enemies.

After Moses died, God made Joshua the leader of the Israelites. Then God said, "Get the people ready to cross over the Jordan River and go into the promised land."

So early the next morning, Joshua and all the Israelites traveled to the Jordan River. On the other side of the river was the promised land—the land of Canaan (KAY nuhn). They camped there for three days.

Then Joshua said, "Make yourselves clean. God is going to do great things tomorrow."

God told Joshua to have the priests carry the ark of the covenant (sometimes called the ark of God) and stand in the water at the edge of the Jordan River. Then Joshua said to the people, "God is here with us. He will defeat our enemies for us. When the priests carrying the ark stand in the river, the waters will stop."

So the priests carried the ark to the river. As soon as their feet touched the water's edge, the water stopped and stood up on one side of them. Then the Israelites crossed the Jordan River on dry ground!

After everyone had crossed, God told Joshua to choose one man from each of the 12 tribes of Israel. Each man was to take a stone from the middle of the river and set it down where the Israelites would spend the night. After the men took the stones from the river, the priests carrying the ark of the covenant crossed over to the other side. As soon as their feet stepped out of the riverbed, the waters started to flow again.

Joshua set up the 12 stones. Then he said to the Israelites, "When your children ask their fathers, 'What do these stones mean?' tell them how Israel crossed the Jordan on dry ground. For God dried up the waters of the Jordan just as He did at the Red Sea. This is so that all the people of the earth will know that the Lord is mighty."

**Christ Connection:** God told Joshua and the Israelites to set up memorial stones to remember what God had done to bring them into the promised land. On the night He died, Jesus told His disciples to remember the sacrifice He was going to make to save us from our sins. When Christians eat the Lord's Supper, they remember God's plan to destroy sin through Jesus' death and resurrection (1 Corinthians 11:26).

**Big Picture Question:** What should God's people remember?

**Big Picture Answer:** God's people should remember all He has done for them and all He promises to do.

# The Conquest of Jericho

The Israelites were camping near the Jordan River. On the other side was the land of Canaan (KAY nuhn)—the land God had promised to give them! All they had to do was take it. But first, the Israelites had to defeat the people who lived there.

Joshua sent 2 spies into the city of Jericho. They stayed at the house of a woman named Rahab (RAY hab). The king of Jericho heard the spies were with Rahab and sent men to find them. But Rahab had heard about all that God had done to Pharaoh, and she believed the Lord was God. She wanted to help His people, so she hid the men on her roof.

When it was safe for the spies to leave, Rahab said, "I know the Lord has given you this land. Please be kind to my family since I've been kind to you. When you attack Jericho, don't kill us."

The spies promised to keep Rahab and her family safe. When they left, Rahab tied a bright red rope in her window so the Israelites would know which house was hers.

Now, a great wall went all the way around Jericho. Because the people of Jericho knew the Israelites were nearby, they closed the city up—no one went in or out.

God told Joshua His plan, "Jericho is yours. March around the city once each day for 6 days. Have the priests carry the ark of the covenant. On the seventh day, march around the city 7 times. Then have the priests blow the trumpets. All the people will shout, and the walls of Jericho will fall down. The Israelites can then take the city."

Joshua and the Israelites did just as God said. On the first day, the people marched once around the city. No one spoke a word. They did this every day for 6 days. On the seventh day, they marched around the city 7 times. Then the priests blew their trumpets, and Joshua said, "Shout, for the Lord has given you the city!" The people shouted, and the wall fell down.

The 2 spies hurried to Rahab's house. They brought her out, with all her family. Rahab was saved because she believed in God. Then the Israelites destroyed everything in the city, just as God told them to do.

**Christ Connection:** God gave the city of Jericho to the Israelites. He fought the battle for them and told them not to take anything from the city. God promised to provide for His people's needs. Jesus spoke of God's provision in Matthew 6:33, "Seek first the kingdom of God and His righteousness, and all these things will be provided for you." Jesus meets our greatest need—to be saved from our sin. We can trust Him for our salvation.

**Big Picture Question:** Who fought the battle of Jericho?

**Big Picture Answer:** God fought for His people and handed Jericho over to the Israelites.

When the people of Israel attacked Jericho, God gave them one rule: Destroy every-thing. Keep nothing for yourselves. But one man, Achan (AY kuhn), disobeyed God. God was angry with the Israelites because of Achan.

After the fall of Jericho, Joshua sent men to a city called Ai (AY igh) to spy out the land. They came back and said, "There aren't many people there, so don't send the whole army."

Only about 3,000 men went to Ai. But they were defeated! They ran away from the men of Ai, and about 36 of them were killed. The Israelites were very afraid.

Joshua tore his clothes and fell to the ground before the ark of God. "Why did you bring us across the Jordan River just to have us killed by these people?" Joshua asked. "When the other people of this land hear that we were scared by the men of Ai, they'll attack us!"

God said, "Stand up! Israel has sinned and disobeyed Me. They have taken the things I told them not to. That's why they cannot defeat their enemies. I will no longer be with you until you get rid of the things I told you to destroy."

Then God said, "Tell the people to make themselves clean. In the morning, they will present themselves to Me one tribe at a time. When I pick out a tribe, that tribe should present itself clan by clan. I'll choose one clan, and that clan will come forward family by family. I'll pick one family, and that family will come forward man by man. The one who is caught with the forbidden things must be punished."

The people did as God said. Israel came forward tribe by tribe, clan by clan, family by family, and man by man. Achan was chosen from all the people.

"Tell me what you have done," Joshua said. "Don't hide anything from me."

"It's true," Achan said. "When we went in to Jericho, I took a beautiful cloak, some silver, and a bar of gold. They are buried in the ground in my tent."

Joshua sent messengers to Achan's tent to collect the things. They laid them before Joshua. "Why have you caused trouble for us?" Joshua asked. "Today God will trouble you!" Then Achan and all his family were killed. God was no longer angry with Israel.

**Christ Connection:** The punishment for Achan's sin was death. It seems harsh, but the Bible says that the wages of sin is death (Romans 6:23). Because we sin, we deserve to die too. Jesus came to die in our place. When we confess our sins and trust in Jesus, we are forgiven and saved from spiritual death.

**Big Picture Question:** How does God feel about sin?

**Big Picture Answer:** God hates sin and punishes sin.

God said to Joshua, "Do not be afraid or discouraged. Take all of your men with you and go up to attack Ai. I will give you victory over them. You may keep all of the livestock and treasures for yourselves."

God told Joshua to set up an ambush behind the city. So Joshua selected 30,000 men. He sent them out at night to lie in wait behind the city.

Joshua had a plan: The rest of the army would go with him toward the city. "When they come out against us," Joshua said, "we will run away like we did before. We will lead them away from the city, then the men hiding behind the city will take it over. They will set the city on fire!" It was the perfect plan.

Early the next morning, Joshua and his men went out toward the city. The king of Ai sent his men out to fight them. When the enemy army got near, Joshua and the Israelites pretended to run away in fear. The army of Ai followed them. The city of Ai was left completely unprotected.

God said to Joshua, "Hold out your sword toward Ai, for I will hand the city over to you."

Joshua held out his sword, and the Israelites hiding behind the city ran in. They set it on fire.

The men of Ai saw that their city was burning behind them. The Israelites in front of them stopped running away and turned back to fight. The army of Ai was trapped! The Israelites had moved in on both sides of them. There was no way to escape. All the people of Ai were struck down.

The Israelites took for themselves the livestock and all the goods in the city, as God had told them to do.

Joshua built an altar to the Lord. He built it just as it was written in the book of the law of Moses. The Israelites sacrificed offerings to God, and Joshua read aloud the words of the law. Everyone heard the laws—from the women to the little children to the foreigners who were with them.

**Christ Connection:** The Israelites were under a covenant in which their obedience directly related to God's presence with them. We are under a new covenant through Jesus Christ, who took the punishment for our sin on Himself. Because of Christ, we are in right standing with God. We are victorious over our enemies because of our faith in Christ (Romans 8:37).

**Big Picture Question:** What does God do when we obey Him?

**Big Picture Answer:** God blesses people who obey Him.

# The Day the Sun Stood Still

Joshua 9; 10:1-15

Joshua and the Israelites had defeated Jericho and Ai (AY igh). They made peace with the people of Gibeon (GIB ih uhn), because the Gibeonites tricked them. They had pretended to be from a faraway land, when they were really Israel's neighbors. When Joshua learned of the trick, he made the Gibeonites servants of Israel.

Now the king of Jerusalem heard about this. He was very afraid because Gibeon was a great city, and all its men were warriors. The Gibeonites and the Israelites were now on the same side!

The king of Jerusalem called to the 4 other kings in the land. He said to them, "Come and help me. We'll attack Gibeon, because they've made peace with Joshua and the Israelites." So the 5 kings joined forces. They went up with all their armies and started a war against Gibeon.

The men of Gibeon sent a message to Joshua: "Help us! Save us! All the kings of this land are at war with us." So Joshua and his whole army went to Gibeon to help them fight.

The Lord said to Joshua, "Don't be afraid, for I have handed them over to you. Not one of them will be able to stand against you."

Joshua and his army marched all night to get to Gibeon. The Israelites surprised the 5 kings' armies. Then the Lord confused them, so that Joshua and his men defeated them. As the king's armies fled, the Lord threw huge hailstones from the sky, killing the men as they ran away. More men died from the hailstones than the Israelites' swords!

But the battle was not over. Joshua needed more time to fight before the sun went down. Joshua prayed to God so that all the Israelites could hear him. He said, "Sun, stand still over Gibeon, and moon, over the valley of Aijalon (A juh lahn)."

God heard Joshua's prayer, and the sun and moon stood still until Israel defeated her enemies. The sun stopped in the middle of the day and didn't set for almost a full day! There has never been a day like that before or since. It was a day when God listened to the voice of man and fought for the Israelites.

**Christ Connection:** Joshua's name means "Yahweh is salvation." God fought for Joshua and the Israelites, saving them and giving them victory over their enemies. God brought us salvation by sending His Son Jesus to die on the cross, giving us victory over sin and death.

**Big Picture Question:** What does God do when we pray?

**Big Picture Answer:** God answers the prayers of His people and saves them.

# Joshua Spoke to the People

Many years had passed since Joshua and the Israelites had defeated Jericho, Ai, and the kings of the land. Joshua was getting old. He gathered the people together and said, "You've seen everything the Lord has done—He has fought your battles for you. The rest of this land will be yours too. God will drive out the people who live there. Then you can take the land, just as God promised you."

"But," Joshua said, "be careful to obey everything that is written in the law of Moses. Don't mix with the nations in this land or worship their gods. Be faithful to God and love Him. If you turn away from God, He won't help you win your battles, and you'll lose this land."

Joshua also said, "I'm going to die soon. You know that God has kept every one of His promises. So know this, too: if you disobey God, He will keep His promise to bring bad things upon you."

Then Joshua reminded the Israelites of all that God had done for them in the past. He told them of Abraham and Isaac, and of Jacob and Esau. He reminded them of how Moses and Aaron had been sent to rescue the Israelites. He told them about the plagues and the parting of the Red Sea. Joshua also spoke about the many battles they had won because God was fighting for them. God had done so many great things for His people!

Then Joshua said, "Get rid of the gods your fathers worshipped in Egypt and worship the Lord. You must choose for yourselves the one you will worship: the gods your fathers worshipped or the Lord. As for me and my family, we will worship the Lord."

The people said, "We know how much God has done for us. We will worship the Lord."

Joshua warned the people, "If you do abandon God to worship other gods, He will turn against you and destroy you!"

"No!" the people replied. "We will worship the Lord!"

Then Joshua wrote these things in the book of the law of God. He also took a large stone and set it up next to the tabernacle of the Lord. "This stone," he said, "will be a reminder to you to serve the Lord." Then Joshua sent the people away. Each man went to the land he had been given.

**Christ Connection:** Joshua was God's chosen servant to bring the Israelites into the promised land. Joshua was a faithful leader who brought the Israelites to a time of peace and physical rest. Joshua reminds of us Jesus. Jesus was chosen by God to be the Savior of the world. He was a servant who gives us the promise of eternal spiritual rest with Him in heaven.

**Big Picture Question:** How can we show our love and faithfulness to God?

**Big Picture Answer:** We can serve, worship, and obey God.

# The First Judges

Joshua had died. Without a strong leader, the Israelites began to disobey God and worship false gods and idols. God was very angry. He let an enemy king take over the Israelites, and they served that king for 8 years.

Then the Israelites cried out to God, "Save us!" So God raised up Othniel (OTH nee uhl) to rule over Israel as their first judge. Othniel led the Israelites into battle against the enemy king, and God helped the Israelites win. The land was peaceful for 40 years, but then Othniel died.

Israel forgot about God again. So God let the king of Moab attack and defeat the Israelites. The Israelites served Moab for 18 years. They remembered how good it had been when they loved and obeyed God, so they cried out to God for help again. God raised up Ehud (EE huhd) to save them. He was a left-handed man from the tribe of Benjamin.

The Israelites sent Ehud to the king of Moab, who was a very fat man. Ehud had a double-edged sword hidden under his clothes. He said to the king, "I have a secret message for you." The king sent all his servants away so that he was alone with Ehud.

When the king stood up from his throne, Ehud pulled out his sword with his left hand and plunged it into the king's belly! The sword was swallowed up by the king's fat—Ehud didn't even pull it out!

Ehud escaped out the porch, locking the doors of the room behind him. When the king's servants came back, Ehud was already gone. The door was locked, and the servants thought the king was using the bathroom. They waited, but the king never opened the door. The servants got worried, so they unlocked the door and found their king dead on the floor!

When Ehud escaped, he blew a ram's horn to call the people to him. "Follow me!" he said. "The Lord has given your enemies to you." So the Israelites battled the Moabites and won. There was peace in the land for 80 years.

When Ehud died, the Israelites forgot God yet again. God gave the Philistines power over Israel. Then they remembered God and cried out to Him, "Save us!" So God sent a third judge, Shamgar (SHAM gahr), to save them.

**Christ Connection:** The judges saved the people from the consequences of their sin, but not the cause of it. God's plan was to one day send a true Deliverer—Jesus, His own Son—to be the King of His people. Jesus would save the people from sin forever.

**Big Picture Question:** How does God make His plan happen?

**Big Picture Answer:** God works in the lives of people to bring about His plan for saving them.

# Deborah and Barak

Othniel, Ehud, and Shamgar had been judges over Israel. After they died, the Israelites forgot about God. So God allowed the king of Canaan to defeat them. The commander of the king's army was named Sisera (SIS uh ruh).

Sisera was cruel to the Israelites for 20 years. The people remembered how good things had been when they loved and obeyed God. So they cried out to God, "Save us!"

Deborah was the judge over Israel at that time. So Deborah called for Barak (BAY rak), the army's leader. She said to him, "Hasn't God told you to lead 10,000 men to Mount Tabor? The Lord will help you defeat Sisera there."

But Barak said, "If you'll go with me, I'll go. But if you won't go with me, I will not go."

"I'll go with you," Deborah said. "But the Lord will give Sisera's defeat to a woman." So Deborah, Barak, and 10,000 men went to Mount Tabor.

When Sisera heard that Barak was at Mount Tabor, he took his 900 iron chariots and all his men to fight.

Deborah said to Barak, "Go! This is the day that God will help you defeat Sisera." So Barak and his 10,000 men moved down the mountain toward Sisera and his army.

The Lord confused Sisera and all his army. Barak chased after them, and everyone in the army was killed by the sword. Not one of them lived—except Sisera, who had left his chariot and run away on foot.

Sisera went to the tent of Jael (JAY uhl), who was the wife of an ally. Jael said, "Come in, my lord. Don't be afraid." Then she gave Sisera some milk to drink and covered him with a rug. Sisera was so tired that he fell into a deep sleep.

Jael knew that Sisera was an evil man and an enemy of God. She took a tent peg and a hammer, and silently crept up to Sisera. Then she hammered the tent peg through Sisera's head and into the ground! She killed him while he slept!

Barak came looking for Sisera. Jael went out to him and said, "I'll show you the man you're looking for." Barak followed her into the tent and saw Sisera lying dead with a tent peg through his head.

That day, God helped the Israelites to defeat the king of Canaan. There was peace for 40 years.

**Christ Connection:** God does what is for His glory and our good (Psalm 115:3; Romans 8:28). God fought for the Israelites and used Deborah, Barak, and Jael to defeat Canaan. In a similar way, God uses people and events to save us not only from our enemies, but to bring about our ultimate good: salvation through His Son, Jesus Christ.

**Big Picture Question:** What is the goal of God's plan?

**Big Picture Answer:** God's goal is to do what is good for us and bring glory to His Name.

# Gideon

The Israelites turned away from God yet again! So God handed them over to be ruled by Midian (MID ee uhn) for 7 years. The Midianites stole their crops and food and left them nothing to eat. They also took the Israelites' sheep, oxen, and donkeys. Israel became very poor. They remembered how good things had been when they loved and obeyed God. So they cried out to God, "Save us!"

The Angel of the Lord then appeared to a man named Gideon and said, "The Lord is with you, mighty warrior!"

At that moment, Gideon was hiding and threshing out some wheat. The Angel's words frightened him. He didn't feel like a mighty warrior. He was the youngest son of the weakest family in his tribe. How could he deliver Israel? But God said, "I will be with you."

Gideon called for all the men to get ready to fight the Midianites. But before he went to battle, Gideon wanted a sign from God.

"I'll put a fleece on the ground," Gideon said. "If the fleece is wet with dew, but the ground is dry, I'll believe You are with me." And that's exactly what happened. The fleece was so wet, Gideon squeezed out enough water to fill a bowl! Then Gideon asked for another sign. This time, the fleece was dry and the ground was wet.

So Gideon and his men prepared for the battle. But God said, "You have too many men. Tell those who are afraid to go home." Many men left—only 10,000 stayed to fight.

"That's still too many," God said. So He made a test for them. All the men went to the river for a drink. Anyone who lapped up the water with his tongue was sent home, but whoever scooped up the water with his hand could stay. Three hundred men were left.

The next day, Gideon and his 300 men surrounded the Midianite camp. They carried trumpets, torches, and pitchers. At Gideon's signal, they blew their trumpets and shattered the pitchers. God turned the Midianites against each other, and the Midianite army ran away. Gideon and his men chased after them and killed the kings of Midian.

The Israelites said to Gideon, "Rule over us, because you saved us from the Midianites."

"I won't rule over you," Gideon said. "God will." But after Gideon died, the Israelites once again worshiped false gods.

**Christ Connection:** The Israelites cried out to God because they knew they could not save themselves. Even Gideon was not enough to save them; God used Gideon to save His people but God fought the battle for them. The people needed someone who was adequate to save. Jesus Christ came to save us from sin because we cannot save ourselves. Only God, through Christ, can save us.

**Big Picture Question:** How should we answer when God asks us to do something?

**Big Picture Answer:** We should obey God and trust Him to help us.

# Samson

The Israelites disobeyed God again, so God handed them over to the Philistines for 40 years. But Manoah (muh NOH uh) and his wife still worshipped God. One day, the Angel of the Lord appeared and told Manoah's wife that she would have a son. "Never cut his hair," He said, "because he will be a Nazirite (NAZ uh rit). He will save Israel from the Philistines."

Manoah's wife did have a son, and she named him Samson. God gave him great strength. When Samson grew up, he wanted to marry a Philistine woman. As he traveled to town to marry her, he found a lion's carcass with a swarm of bees and honey inside. So Samson told this riddle to the Philistines: *Out of the eater came something to eat, and out of the strong came something sweet.*

Samson was talking about the honey, but the Philistines couldn't solve the riddle. They threatened to kill Samson's new wife if she didn't help them. Samson's wife cried until he told her the answer, then she told the men. Samson was angry and left his wife. He went back to get her later, but her father had given her to another man.

Samson was so angry that he tied torches to the tails of 300 foxes. Then he turned them loose in the Philistines' fields, burning them up. When the Philistines tried to capture Samson, he killed 1,000 men with a donkey's jawbone!

Later, Samson fell in love with Delilah. The Philistines offered Delilah lots of money if she would tell them the secret of Samson's strength.

So Delilah asked Samson, "What makes you so strong? How can you be tied?" Samson said he could be tied with fresh bowstring and new ropes. But these didn't work. Delilah nagged and nagged Samson until he said, "If you cut my hair, I'll lose my strength."

Delilah called for the Philistines. While Samson slept, they cut his hair. Delilah woke Samson, saying, "The Philistines are here to kill you!" Samson tried to fight, but his strength was gone.

The Philistines blinded Samson and threw him in prison, where his hair began to grow back. One day, the Philistines stood Samson between 2 pillars in the temple of their god Dagon. Samson cried out to God, "Please strengthen me once more." God did, and Samson pushed on the pillars until the temple collapsed. Samson and all the Philistines inside died.

**Christ Connection:** God raised up Samson as the last judge to deliver the Israelites from the Philistines. Samson killed more Philistines in his death than he did in his life. Jesus would come as the last Deliverer, saving through His life and His death those who would trust in Him.

**Big Picture Question:** What should I do when I sin?

**Big Picture Answer:** I should ask God to forgive me.

During the time of the judges, a woman named Naomi (nay OH mee) lived in Bethlehem with her husband, Elimelech (ee LIM ee lek), and their 2 sons. There was a famine in the land, so they traveled to Moab where there was food.

While they were in Moab, Elimelech died. Naomi's sons married Moabite women, Orpah (OR puh) and Ruth. Then Naomi's sons died too! Naomi heard that the famine had ended in Bethlehem, so she decided to return home. She told Orpah and Ruth to go back to their own families.

Weeping, Orpah kissed her mother-in-law goodbye and left. But Ruth clung to Naomi and said. "Wherever you go, I will go, and wherever you live, I will live. Your people will be my people, and your God will be my God."

Naomi and Ruth traveled to Bethlehem. It was the beginning of the barley harvest, so Ruth went into the fields to gather the grain that the workers dropped. This would be their food. She happened to go to the field of Boaz, a good man from the family of Elimelech.

Boaz saw Ruth and asked who she was. When he found out she was Naomi's daughter-in-law, he said to her, "Don't go to any other fields. Stay here with my servants where you'll be safe." Then he made sure Ruth had enough food.

"Why are you so kind?" Ruth asked.

"I've heard about all you've done for Naomi," he told her.

Ruth told Naomi about Boaz. "He's one of our family redeemers," Naomi said. (A family redeemer was someone who would help his relatives if they were in trouble.) Naomi told Ruth to keep working in his fields.

Now, Naomi wanted Ruth to have a husband to care for her. At the end of the harvest, she told Ruth to put on her best clothes. Then she sent Ruth to the threshing floor to lie down at Boaz's feet. In this way, Ruth showed him that she hoped he would marry her. Boaz did promise to marry her. He filled her shawl with grain and sent her back to Naomi.

Boaz bought back the land that had belonged to Naomi's husband, and then he married Ruth. They had a son named Obed, and Naomi took care of him. When Obed grew up, he became the father of Jesse, who was the father of King David.

**Christ Connection:** Boaz was a family redeemer. That means he would help any of his relatives who were in trouble. Boaz cared for Ruth and Naomi because their husbands had died. In a similar way, Jesus is our Redeemer. We need help because we sin. Jesus bought our salvation for us by taking our punishment when He died on the cross.

**Big Picture Question:** Who is our redeemer?

**Big Picture Answer:** Jesus is our redeemer because He saves us from our sins.

There was a man named Elkanah (el KAY nah), who lived with his 2 wives, Hannah and Peninnah (pih NIN ah). Peninnah was mean to Hannah because God had not given her any children.

Every year, Elkanah went to the tabernacle to worship God. Hannah and Peninnah went with him. And every year, Peninnah would tease Hannah until she wept. Hannah went to the tabernacle and prayed to God. Weeping with many tears, she promised, "Lord, if You give me a son, he will serve You all his life."

Eli, the priest, was sitting nearby. He couldn't hear her, but he saw her lips moving. Eli thought she was drunk and scolded her.

But Hannah said, "My heart is broken. I've been pouring out my heart to the Lord."

So Eli said, "Go in peace. May God answer your prayers."

Hannah returned home, and God did answer her prayers. She had a son, and she named him Samuel. When Samuel was no longer a baby, Hannah took him to Eli at the tabernacle. She reminded Eli of who she was.

"God gave me this boy," she said, "and now I give him to the Lord." Hannah went back home and left Samuel with Eli to serve God. Every year, she made Samuel a new robe and took it to him. God gave Hannah 3 more sons and 2 daughters.

Now, Eli was very old. His sons were also priests, but they were wicked men who sinned against God. Samuel pleased God, though.

One night, the Lord called to Samuel. Samuel thought Eli had called him. He ran to Eli, saying, "Here I am!"

But Eli said, "I didn't call you. Go back and lie down."

Twice more, the Lord called to Samuel, and twice more Samuel ran to Eli. After the third time, Eli finally understood that God was the one calling Samuel. He told Samuel what to say.

Once again God called, "Samuel, Samuel!"

This time Samuel answered, "Speak, for Your servant is listening."

Then God told Samuel that He was going to judge Eli's sons for their sins. The next day, Eli asked what God had said. Samuel was afraid to tell him, but Eli insisted. Then Eli said, "He is the Lord. He will do what He thinks is good."

As Samuel grew, God was with him. Everyone in Israel knew that Samuel was God's messenger.

**Christ Connection:** Samuel became a prophet to the nation of Israel. He used God's words to tell the people what God is like. John 1:1 says that Jesus is the Word. God sent Jesus to earth as God in the flesh. Jesus showed the world what God is like, and He told people to turn away from their sin. Jesus ultimately gave sinful people the power to stop sinning by dying for their sins on the cross and rising again.

**Big Picture Question:** Who spoke to Samuel?

**Big Picture Answer:** God spoke to Samuel, and Samuel listened.

# The Ark Was Captured

The Philistines were enemies of the people of Israel. The Israelites went to battle against the Philistines, but the Philistines won, killing about 4,000 Israelites.

"Why did God let us lose this battle?" asked the leaders of Israel. In the past, God had helped them defeat their enemies.

But instead of asking God what they had done wrong, the Israelites decided to take the ark of God—sometimes called the ark of the covenant—and carry it to the battlefield. (Now, the ark of God was a wooden box covered in gold that reminded them God was with His people.)

Eli's sons were priests, and they had the ark of God. But they were also very wicked. They did not ask God to help them fight. Instead, they just took the ark of God to the Israelites' camp. When the Israelite army saw the ark, they shouted so loudly that the ground shook. Surely they would win the battle now!

The Philistines heard the shout, but they didn't know what was happening. When they heard that the Israelites had the ark of God, they panicked! They could fight against men, but who could fight against God?

But the Philistines did fight—and they won again! They killed thousands of Israelites, including Eli's sons. But worst of all, they stole the ark of God! One of the Israelite soldiers escaped the battle and ran to tell Eli the priest what had happened. When Eli heard the news, he fell backward off his chair, broke his neck, and died.

The Philistines took the ark of God to a temple where they worshipped Dagon (DAY gahn), a false god. They put the ark next to a statue of Dagon. The next morning, the Philistines found that Dagon's statue had fallen facedown in front of the ark of God. They set the statue back in its place. But the next day, it was facedown again. This time, the head and hands were broken off.

The Philistines moved the ark to another city, but the people there became very sick. The ark was moved again, and again the people got sick. Wherever the ark of God was taken, God punished the people living in that city. The Philistines were afraid. They didn't want God to punish them anymore, so they decided to send the ark of God back to the Israelites, where it belonged.

**Christ Connection:** The ark of God was important to the Israelites because it reminded God's people that God was with them. Years later, God gave His people something greater than a sign that He was with them; God gave them His Son Jesus—God in the flesh. One of Jesus' names is Immanuel, which means "God with us."

**Big Picture Question:** Why was the ark of God important?

**Big Picture Answer:** The ark reminded God's people that God was with them.

# Israel Demanded a King

For many years, Israel had been ruled by judges. At that time, Samuel was the judge over Israel. Because he was growing old, he made his two sons—Joel and Abijah (uh BI juh)—judges over Israel. But they were not honest or fair.

The leaders of Israel went to Samuel and said, "We don't want your sons to lead us. We want a king!" All the other nations around Israel had kings, and the Israelites wanted one too.

Samuel prayed to God. "Give the people what they want," God said. "They're not rejecting you. They're rejecting Me as their king. Give them what they want, but warn them what it will be like to have an earthly king."

Samuel told the people what God had said. Then he warned, "A king will take your sons for his army and your daughters for his servants. He will take a part of your crops and your flocks. Even you yourselves may become his servants. One day you will cry out because of the king you've chosen, but God won't answer you."

But the people wouldn't listen. "Give us a king!" they cried.

So God said, "Give them a king."

Meanwhile, a wealthy man named Kish was looking for some missing donkeys. Kish sent his son Saul with a servant to search for them. Now Saul was handsome and tall—he was a head taller than anyone else.

Saul and the servant searched for the donkeys, but couldn't find them. Saul was ready to give up, when his servant said, "There's a man of God in this city. Maybe he can tell us which way we should go."

They found the man of God—and it was Samuel! Now God had told Samuel that Saul would be coming and that he should anoint him as king. So Samuel said, "Don't worry about the donkeys. They've been found." Then he invited Saul to eat with him.

The next morning, Samuel told Saul that God had chosen him to be king of Israel. He poured oil out on Saul's head to anoint him as king. Then Saul went home, and the Spirit of God was with him.

Later, Samuel gathered the Israelites to present Saul as their new king, but they couldn't find him! God said, "He's hidden among the supplies." The people ran to get Saul.

"Long live the king!" they shouted.

**Christ Connection:** The Israelites demanded a king, so Samuel anointed Saul. It wasn't wrong for the Israelites to want a king; God intended for a king to rule over them. But the Israelites had rejected God. They didn't trust God to rule over them. God had a plan to one day send His Son, Jesus, to rule over Israel. Jesus would be their perfect King and would bring them peace and salvation.

**Big Picture Question:** What king of king did God plan to give Israel?

**Big Picture Answer:** God planned to send a perfect king—Jesus Christ.

# God Rejected Saul as King

As king of Israel, Saul gathered an army to fight their enemies, the Philistines. Some of the men went with Saul into the hill country, and the rest went with Saul's son Jonathan to a place called Gibeah (GIB ee uh).

Jonathan led his men to attack and destroy a Philistine army camp. The Philistines then gathered their army together to fight Israel. Saul sent messengers throughout Israel, calling for more men to help fight.

The Philistines had 3,000 chariots, 6,000 men on horseback, and more foot soldiers than anyone could count! When the Israelites saw them, they were afraid. They hid in caves, thickets, and holes.

Samuel had told Saul to wait for him for 7 days, then Samuel would come and tell Saul what he should do. Saul waited, but Samuel didn't come. Saul's soldiers began to leave him. Not wanting to wait any longer, Saul made an offering to God. (This was a sin! Saul was the king, not the priest. Only the priest could offer a sacrifice.) Saul had just finished the offering when Samuel came.

"What have you done?" Samuel asked.

"The men were leaving me! I wanted to ask for God's help to fight the Philistines," Saul answered.

"You have disobeyed God," Samuel said. "You will not be king much longer. God is going to find someone who will obey Him to be king."

Some time later, Samuel came to Saul with a message from God. God wanted Saul to attack the Amalekites (uh MAL uh kaits) and destroy all their people and animals. So Saul and his army fought the Amalekites and won. But they didn't destroy everything as God said. Saul only destroyed the worthless things he didn't want.

God told Samuel, "I am sorry that I made Saul king because he does not obey Me."

Samuel told Saul what God had said.

"I did obey Him!" Saul argued. "I only saved the best animals to sacrifice to God."

"Does God care more about obedience or sacrifices?" Samuel asked. "You rejected God's word, so God has rejected you as king."

"I have sinned," Saul said. "Please forgive me!"

But Samuel said, "God has taken away your kingship today; He is giving it to another king."

**Christ Connection:** God's message to Saul was clear: Obey Me and all will go well for you. But Saul did not obey God. Samuel told Saul he would not last as king. God rejected Saul as king, but He had a plan to bring Jesus—His Son and our perfect King—to rule over His people forever.

**Big Picture Question:** How does God feel when His people obey?

**Big Picture Answer:** God is happy when we obey Him, but all of us sin and need a Savior.

Because Saul had disobeyed God, Israel needed a new king. God told Samuel to visit a man in Bethlehem named Jesse. Jesse had 8 sons, and one of them would be Israel's new king.

So Samuel went to Bethlehem. He first saw Jesse's oldest son, Eliab (ee LYE ab), who was tall and handsome. This must be God's chosen king! Samuel thought.

"No, Samuel," God said. "You can only see what is on the outside, but I can see the heart."

One by one, Jesse's sons came to Samuel, but God didn't choose any of them.

"Do you have any more sons?" Samuel asked.

"My youngest son, David, is out taking care of the sheep," Jesse said, and he sent for David.

When David arrived, God said, "He's the one!" Then Samuel poured oil on David's head and the Spirit of the Lord was with him.

But the Spirit of the Lord left Saul, and God sent an evil spirit to torment him. Saul's servants thought that music might help him feel better. One servant knew just the right person to play for the king—David! So whenever Saul felt troubled, David would come and play his harp.

At this time, the Philistines got ready to attack Israel. Saul sent his army out to meet them. The Israelites camped on one hill and the Philistines camped on another, with a valley between them.

The Philistines had a warrior named Goliath. He was 9 feet 9 inches tall! Goliath shouted to the Israelites, "Send me your best man, and we'll fight one-on-one." But no one wanted to fight Goliath!

Jesse sent David to check on his 3 oldest sons, who were in the Israelite army. David saw Goliath and watched the Israelites run away in fear. Then David said he would fight Goliath.

"You can't fight Goliath!" Saul said.

But David said, "God will keep me safe."

Saul offered his armor to David, but it was too big. So David took only his slingshot and 5 smooth stones. Then he went out to meet Goliath. Goliath laughed at David because he was just a boy. But David said, "You fight with a spear and sword, but I fight in the name of God!"

Then David ran toward Goliath. He took out a stone, slung it, and hit Goliath right in the forehead! Goliath fell facedown. With God's help, David had won!

**Christ Connection:** The Israelites were up against their toughest enemies, the Philistines. They didn't stand a chance against Goliath, the mighty Philistine warrior. God gave David power to defeat Goliath. David reminds us of Jesus, who came to save us from our greatest enemies: sin and death. When we look to Jesus, the ultimate hero, He gives us salvation and eternal life.

**Big Picture Question:** Who gave David the power to defeat Goliath?

**Big Picture Answer:** God gave David the power to defeat Goliath.

# David and Jonathan

1 Samuel 18:1-11; 19:1-7; 20:1-42

After David killed Goliath, he went to live at Saul's palace. There he became best friends with Saul's son, Jonathan.

David was successful at everything Saul asked him to do, and Saul made David an officer in his army. But the people seemed to like David better than Saul. Saul became so jealous that he tried to kill David! He even ordered Jonathan to kill David! But Jonathan was David's friend. He warned David, saying, "Go hide until I can talk to my father."

The next morning, Jonathan asked Saul, "Why do you want to kill David? He's done nothing but help you." Saul agreed and promised not to kill David. But Saul didn't keep his promise for long. One day, when David was playing the harp for him, Saul threw a spear at him. David escaped and told Jonathan what had happened.

"That can't be true!" Jonathan said. "My father would tell me if he wanted you dead."

"It's true," David replied. "Your father knows we're friends. That's why he didn't tell you."

"How can I help?" Jonathan asked.

David had a plan. "The New Moon festival is tomorrow. I'm supposed to eat with the king, but I'm not going. If Saul asks where I am, tell him I went to Bethlehem. If he gets angry, you'll know he wants to kill me."

David went to hide in a field. After the festival, Jonathan would signal David by shooting 3 arrows into the field. If it were safe for David to return, Jonathan would send his servant to get the arrows, saying, "The arrows are to the side of you!" But if Saul wanted to kill David, Jonathan would say, "The arrows are beyond you!"

So Jonathan went to the feast. When Saul sat down to eat, he asked, "Where's David?"

"He's in Bethlehem," Jonathan said.

Saul was furious, and he yelled, "David deserves to die!" Then he threw his spear at Jonathan! Jonathan knew then that Saul wanted to kill David.

The next morning, Jonathan went to the field and shot 3 arrows. As his servant went to get them, Jonathan shouted, "The arrows are beyond you!" David knew Saul wanted to kill him.

Jonathan sent his servant away, and David came out of hiding. David and Jonathan wept as they said good-bye. The 2 men parted, but they knew they would always be friends.

**Christ Connection:** Jonathan was a true friend to David. Everyone could use a friend like that! Jonathan's life gives us a glimpse of Jesus, the mighty friend of sinners. Jesus calls us friends (John 15:15). He gave up His position in heaven to come down to us, gave up His life to save us, and intercedes for us before God.

**Big Picture Question:** Who is our friend?

**Big Picture Answer:** Jesus is our friend—no matter what.

God chose David to be king of Israel. When David was young, he had played the harp for King Saul, and God had given him the power to defeat Goliath, the great Philistine warrior. When David became king, God gave His people a time of peace.

One day, David was talking with Nathan, who was a prophet of God. David said, "I live in a house of nice cedar wood, but the ark of God sits inside a tent!" It didn't seem right to David. He wanted to build a temple for the ark of God. He told Nathan his plans.

"God is with you. Do what you want!" Nathan said. But God didn't want David to build him a house. That night, God gave Nathan a message for David. This is what God wanted Nathan to say:

"David, are you going to build a house for Me to live in? From the time I brought the Israelites out of Egypt until today, I have lived in a tent. I have never said to anyone, 'Why haven't you built a house for me?'"

"David, I took you from the pasture where you watched the sheep. I made you king. I've been with you wherever you have gone. I've defeated your enemies for you. I will make your name great. And when you die, one of your sons will be king. He will be a strong king, and no one will be able to take his kingdom away from him. Your son will build a house for Me. I will love him, and I will never leave him. Your throne will last forever."

Nathan told David everything God said. David then went into the tent he had set up for the ark of God. He sat down and prayed:

"Lord God, I don't deserve anything You have done for me, and You promise to do so much more! God, You are so great! There is no one like You! You chose the Israelites to be Your own people. You rescued them from slavery in Egypt.

"God, please keep Your promises to me and my family. I know You will keep Your promises because You always do."

**Christ Connection:** God made David a promise that would last forever! God told David that every future king of Israel would come from David's family, and David's kingdom would last forever. God kept His promise by sending His Son, Jesus, to be one of David's descendants. Jesus is our King who will never die; He will rule over God's people forever.

**Big Picture Question:** What did God promise David?

**Big Picture Answer:** God promised that David's kingdom would last forever.

# David Sinned and Was Restored

2 Samuel 11:1–12:14; Psalm 51

David was king of Israel. In the springtime, kings often led their armies to war. But one spring, David put Joab (JOH ab) in charge of his army. Then he sent them out to fight the Ammonites (AM uh naits), while David stayed in Jerusalem.

One evening, David was walking on the roof of his palace when he saw Bathsheba. She was the wife of Uriah (yoo RI uh), one of David's best warriors, and she was very beautiful. David had Bathsheba brought to his palace. Then later, Bathsheba told David that she was going to have his baby.

David didn't want anyone to find out that Bathsheba's baby was his. So he called Uriah home from the battle and told him to spend time with his wife. But Uriah didn't think it was right to relax at home while his men were at war. He slept on David's doorstep and did not see his wife.

So David came up with another plan. He told Joab to send Uriah into the hottest part of the battle, so that he would be killed. Joab did as David said, and Uriah died. When Bathsheba heard the news, she was very sad. David took Bathsheba into his house to be his wife, and she gave birth to a baby boy.

David thought he had gotten away with it, but God knew what David had done. He sent Nathan the prophet to tell David a story:

*"A rich man and a poor man lived in the same city. The rich man had many animals, but the poor man only had one little lamb, which he loved. A traveler came to the rich man. And instead of offering one of his own animals to the traveler, the rich man took the poor man's lamb and killed it for the traveler to eat."*

David was angry. "The rich man should die!" he said.

"You are that man!" Nathan said. Then Nathan told him that God had given him everything he needed, but David had killed Uriah to take his wife. David knew then that he deserved to die for his sin.

But Nathan said, "You won't die for this, but God will punish you. Your son will die instead."

After that, David wrote a psalm. He confessed his sin and asked God to restore him. "God, create a clean heart for me," David prayed.

**Christ Connection:** When David sinned against God, God forgave him, but sin always comes with a price. God spared David's life, but David's son died because of David's sin. When we sin, we can receive God's forgiveness because God sent His Son Jesus to pay the price for our sin. Jesus died the death we deserve so that we could be made right with God.

**Big Picture Question:** What happened when David sinned?

**Big Picture Answer:** God punished David, but He also forgave him.

David had been king over Israel for a long time, but now he was growing old. It was time for his son Solomon to become king. Because David was at the end of his life, he gave Solomon some advice.

"Be strong and brave, Solomon," David said. "Obey God, and He will give you success in everything you do. God promised that if we are faithful, then every king of Israel will come from our family."

When David died, Solomon took control of his father's kingdom. He married the daughter of Pharaoh, the king of Egypt. With the princess as his wife, Solomon didn't have to worry about being attacked by the Egyptians. So the two countries were at peace.

One night, God appeared to Solomon in a dream. God said, "Solomon, ask Me for anything. What should I give you?"

Now Solomon could have asked for power, or riches, or a long life. He could have asked for victory over his enemies. But Solomon didn't ask for any of these things. Solomon wanted to be a good king, so he asked for something even better.

Solomon said, "Lord my God, You have made me king in my father David's place. But I am young, and I don't know very much about being a king. Your people are too many to be counted. Please give me a wise and obedient heart. Help me know the difference between right and wrong. Help me lead Your people well."

God was pleased with Solomon. He said, "I will give you a wise and understanding heart. I will make you wiser than anyone who has ever lived. There will never be anyone as wise as Solomon."

Then God said, "Because you asked for wisdom, I will also give you what you did not ask for: long life, riches, and honor. You'll be greater than any other king."

Solomon woke up and realized God had spoken to him in a dream. Then he went to Jerusalem to worship God and offer sacrifices to Him.

**Christ Connection:** King Solomon could have asked for earthly treasures, but he asked for wisdom to lead God's people. God created people to do His will. Jesus provided the ultimate example by completely trusting God with His life. Jesus wanted to carry out God's plan, and He trusted God to take care of the rest. Jesus ultimately surrendered His own life to die on the cross for our sins so that God could bring us back to Himself.

**Big Picture Question:** What did King Solomon ask from God?

**Big Picture Answer:** King Solomon asked God for wisdom to lead God's people.

# Solomon Built the Temple

Solomon became king of Israel after his father David died. God was with Solomon, and He made Solomon very wise. In Solomon's fourth year as king, he began to build a temple for the Lord. The temple would take the place of the tabernacle where God had met with His people for 480 years—ever since God had led them out of Egypt.

Solomon ordered thousands of workers to help build the temple. The workers cut cedar logs and stone blocks. They laid the foundation and built the outside of the temple.

God blessed the building of the temple and made a promise to Solomon: "If you obey My commands, I will keep the promise I made to your father David. I will live among the Israelites, and I will not leave My people."

It took 7 years to build the temple. The walls were made of stone and covered with boards of cedar. The cedar was carved with beautiful gourds and flower blossoms. The most holy place—where the ark of God was to be set—was completely covered with pure gold!

With God's temple complete, it was time for Solomon to move the ark of God into the new temple in Jerusalem. Solomon gathered the leaders of Israel. As the priests moved the ark, King Solomon and all the people who had gathered offered sacrifices of sheep and cattle to the Lord.

The priests placed the ark of God in the most holy place in the temple. When the priests came out, a cloud filled the temple, and God's glory was in the cloud.

"Praise God!" Solomon said. "God promised my father David that his son would build a temple. God kept His promise!"

Solomon stood before the altar of the Lord and prayed, "Lord, there is no God like You in heaven above or on earth below!"

As Solomon prayed, he thought about the future. He knew Israel would sin again and make God angry. So Solomon asked for forgiveness, and he asked God to hear their prayers.

When Solomon finished praying, he said to the Israelites, "Let your hearts be completely devoted to God. Obey Him in all things." The people offered sacrifices and worshipped God for 14 days. Then they went home with their hearts were full of joy for all that God had done.

**Christ Connection:** The temple Solomon built was a temporary dwelling place, and because God is holy, only the priests could approach God, and only if they followed specific instructions. Ordinary people had no direct access to the living God. Jesus changed all that. By His death on the cross, Jesus took away our sin. We can approach God intimately and individually when we trust Jesus as Lord and Savior.

**Big Picture Question:** What did God promise Solomon?

**Big Picture Answer:** God promised that if Solomon would obey His commands, He would live among His people and never leave them.

89

King Solomon loved God, but he didn't always obey God.

God had warned the Israelites not to marry people from other nations. Those people worshipped false gods, and God knew they would lead the Israelites away from Him. But King Solomon had hundreds of wives, and many of them were from other nations. Solomon began to worship the false gods of his wives. He even built shrines for them!

God was angry. He warned Solomon, but Solomon would not listen. So God said, "I will take this kingdom away from you. You will be king the rest of your life. But when your son becomes king, he will lose everything except for one tribe."

When Solomon died, his son Rehoboam (REE huh BOH uhm) became king. The people told Rehoboam, "Your father Solomon made us work too hard. We will gladly serve you if you make our work easier."

Rehoboam thought about it and he asked his friends about, but he didn't ask God about it. Then he said, "My father Solomon didn't make you work hard enough! I'll make you work even harder!"

This was not the answer God's people were hoping for! The people from the northern tribes didn't want to serve a king like Rehoboam. They went home and made Jeroboam (JER uh BOH uhm) their king. He had been a servant of Solomon. Only the southern tribe of Judah stayed under Rehoboam's rule.

Rehoboam didn't like being the king of only one tribe. He planned to attack the Northern Kingdom of Israel, but God sent a prophet to stop him. The prophet said, "Don't fight them! The people of Israel are your family. Go home!" So Rehoboam went home.

Jeroboam, king of Israel, saw that his people still traveled to Jerusalem to worship God at the temple. He was afraid if they kept going to Jerusalem, they would start thinking of Rehoboam as their king again. So Jeroboam made 2 golden calves.

"Going to Jerusalem is too hard for you," he told the people. "Look! These golden calves are the gods who brought your ancestors out of Egypt. Worship them."

What Jeroboam did was a terrible sin! Those calves didn't lead God's people out of Egypt—God did! Jeroboam even built shrines and led the people in worship to those false gods.

**Christ Connection:** King Solomon's sin led to the division of Israel. Jeroboam led the northern tribes away from God, and Solomon's son, Rehoboam, ruled over the southern tribes. Every king failed at leading God's people well. God's people needed a better king, a perfect king! Through David's family, God would bring His own Son, Jesus Christ, to be king over God's people forever. Jesus would lead the people perfectly back to God.

**Big Picture Question:** How did God punish King Solomon's sin?

**Big Picture Answer:** God divided Israel into 2 kingdoms.

# Poetry and Wisdom

King David loved God, and he wrote many psalms (or songs) about God. The songs that David and others wrote are collected in the book of Psalms.

David wrote psalms of praise and thanks for all the great things God has done. He sang, "Yahweh, our Lord, how magnificent is Your name throughout the earth!" (Psalm 8:1).

David also sang to God when he was sad or afraid. When David was being hunted by his enemies, he sang, "When I am afraid, I will trust in You. In God, whose word I praise, in God I trust; I will not fear" (Psalm 56:3–4).

Even when David sinned, he wrote songs. He told God how sorry he was and asked God to forgive him: "Against You—You alone—I have sinned . . . God, create a clean heart for me" (Psalm 51:4, 9). David understood that God didn't just want sacrifices. God wanted David's heart to change so he would not sin anymore.

David also wrote songs to show how important it is to read and learn God's Word. He thought about God's Word all the time, and he taught his son Solomon to love God's Word too.

When Solomon became king, he asked God for wisdom, so that he would be a good leader for the Israelites. God was pleased, and He gave Solomon so much wisdom that everyone knew God had blessed Solomon.

Solomon used his wisdom to write many wise sayings called *proverbs*. In the book of Proverbs, Solomon told people to love and worship God. He also told people how to make wise decisions. If people would listen to God's words and do what God told them to do, then God would bless and protect them, Solomon wrote. But if they didn't obey God's words, they would make bad decisions and face punishment for their sins. "Trust in the Lord with all your heart," Solomon wrote in Proverbs 3:5.

In the book of Ecclesiastes, Solomon wrote about how God made the world so that people would worship Him and see how good He is. Solomon even wrote a poem that taught there is a time for everything under heaven: "a time to give birth and a time to die . . . a time to weep and a time to laugh; a time to mourn and a time to dance" (Ecclesiastes 3:2–4).

**Christ Connection:** Wisdom in the Bible is not just words about how to live. Romans 8:29 says that God has planned to change people who know and love Jesus to become like Jesus. God gives us wisdom because He wants us to be like Jesus—in how we live, how we speak, and how we think.

**Big Picture Question:** Where does wisdom come from?

**Big Picture Answer:** Wisdom comes from God.

The people of Israel had wanted a king, but their kings were not faithful to God. They led the Israelite people in worshipping false gods and idols. God judged the kings because they led His people away from Him.

Now Baasha (BAY uh shuh) was king of Israel for 24 years. He did what was evil in God's sight and led the people of Israel to sin.

God spoke to the prophet Jehu (JEH hoo) about King Baasha. God said this: "I raised you up and made you ruler over Israel. But you have caused My people to sin. You have made me angry. So I will sweep away Baasha and all his house."

When Baasha died, his son Elah became king in his place. Elah was king for 2 years when Zimri (ZIM ri), the commander of half the king's chariots, began to plot against him. Zimri killed Elah and became king in his place.

As soon as Zimri was seated on his throne, he struck down the entire house of Baasha. He didn't leave a single man or boy alive! But Zimri was king for only 7 days. The army of Israel heard that Zimri had killed King Elah, so they made Omri (OM ri), the army commander, king over Israel. Omri, along with all the Israelite army, marched up and captured the city where Zimri was. When Zimri saw that the city was captured, he went into the royal palace and burned it down over himself.

Omri became king over Israel and reigned for 12 years. But Omri did what was evil in the Lord's sight. He caused Israel to sin by worshipping worthless idols. When Omri died, his son Ahab became king in his place.

Ahab reigned over Israel for 22 years. Ahab was more evil than any of the other kings. He built a temple for the false god Baal (BAY uhl) and worshipped him. Ahab did more to anger the Lord God of Israel than all the kings of Israel who were before him!

**Christ Connection:** God's people asked for a king to lead them, but every king led them away from God. Was there any king on earth who would be faithful? God would send a king from Himself who would lead God's people back to God. He would be the King of all kings—Jesus Christ.

**Big Picture Question:** What kind of king did God's people need?

**Big Picture Answer:** God's people needed a faithful king who loved and obeyed God.

# Elijah Confronted Evil Ahab

Ahab was now king of Israel, but he led the people in worshipping the false god Baal (BAY uhl). So God punished Ahab with a terrible drought for 3 years.

Now Elijah was a prophet of God. One day, God sent Elijah to Ahab with a message: "You have destroyed Israel by worshipping Baal. Tell all of Israel to meet me at Mount Carmel. Bring the 450 prophets of Baal with you."

When the people had gathered, Elijah said, "I am the only prophet of God, but Baal has 450 prophets. Let us each prepare a bull to sacrifice, but not light the fire. You call on Baal, and I'll call on Yahweh. The God who answers with fire is the true God."

So the prophets of Baal prepared their sacrifice, but didn't light the fire. They called on Baal from morning until noon, but there was no answer.

Elijah made fun of them: "Shout louder! Maybe Baal is sleeping!" So they shouted louder, they danced, and they even cut themselves with knives! All day long, they did this, but there was no answer.

Then Elijah built an altar and dug a trench around it. He put the wood and the bull on top. "Fill four water pots and pour the water over the offering," he said. Then he ordered them to do it again . . . and again! The altar was soaked, and water filled the trench.

Elijah said, "Answer me, Lord, so that this people will know You are God!"

Yahweh's fire fell. It burned up the offering, the wood, stones, dust, and even the water in the trench! The people fell facedown and said, "Yahweh, He is God!"

"Seize the prophets of Baal," Elijah ordered, and he killed them all. Then he went to the top of Mount Carmel and bowed down on the ground. He said to his servant, "Go and look toward the sea."

"There's nothing," the servant said. Seven times Elijah sent him back. On the seventh time, he said, "There's a cloud as small as a man's hand."

Then Elijah said, "Tell Ahab to get his chariot ready so the rain doesn't stop him."

The sky grew dark, and there was a terrible downpour. Ahab got in his chariot and headed for Jezreel. But God's power was with Elijah. He tucked up his robes and ran so fast that he passed Ahab in his chariot!

**Christ Connection:** Elijah called on the power of God to prove to the worshippers of Baal that God is the one, true God. By sending fire from heaven, God displayed His great power. God would use His power years later to raise His Son, Jesus, from the dead.

**Big Picture Question:** Who is the one, true God?

**Big Picture Answer:** Yahweh is the one, true God.

King Ahab told his wife, Jezebel (JEZ uh bel), everything that Elijah had done and how he had killed all the prophets of Baal. Now King Ahab was wicked, but Queen Jezebel was even more wicked! She had already killed many of God's prophets. So Jezebel sent a messenger to Elijah, saying, "May the gods punish me if I don't kill you!"

Elijah was afraid and ran for his life. He went a day's journey into the wilderness. There, he sat down under a broom tree and prayed, "I've had enough! Lord, take my life." Then he lay down and slept.

Suddenly, an angel touched him and said, "Get up and eat."

Elijah saw a loaf of bread and a jug of water. So he ate and drank and lay down again. Then the angel of the Lord returned a second time and said, "Get up and eat, or the journey will be too much for you." So Elijah ate and drank. Then on the strength of that food, he walked 40 days and 40 nights to Horeb (HOR uhb), the mountain of God. He went into a cave there and spent the night.

God said, "What are you doing here, Elijah?"

Elijah answered, "The Israelites have torn down Your altars and killed Your prophets. I am the only one left, and they're looking to kill me."

God said, "Go out and stand on the mountain." At that moment, God was passing by. A great and mighty wind tore at the mountain, but God was not in the wind. After the wind there was an earthquake, but God was not in the earthquake. After the earthquake there was a fire, but God was not in the fire. And after the fire there was a voice, a soft whisper. When Elijah heard it, he went out and stood at the entrance of the cave.

A voice said, "What are you doing here, Elijah?"

"I have been very zealous for the Lord God," he answered, "but the Israelites are looking to kill me."

God said, "Go to the Wilderness of Damascus (duh MAS kuhs). When you arrive, anoint Hazael (HAZ uh el) as king over Aram. Then anoint Jehu as king over Israel and Elisha as prophet in your place."

So Elijah left there and found Elisha as he was plowing. Elijah walked by him and threw his cloak over him. Elisha followed Elijah and served him.

**Christ Connection:** Elijah was one of many prophets leading to Jesus, the true and final prophet. Like Elijah, Jesus faced opposition from those who hated Him. Through the death of Jesus, God was victorious over those who oppose Him.

**Big Picture Question:** How does God help in times of trouble?

**Big Picture Answer:** God promises to never leave us.

# Elisha and Naaman

Naaman (NAY uh muhn) was the commander of the army for the king of Aram. He was a brave warrior, but he had a terrible skin disease.

Now Naaman's wife had a young servant girl who was from Israel. The girl said to her mistress, "If only my master would go to the prophet Elisha. He would cure him."

So Naaman told the king of Aram what the girl had said. The king said, "Go and I will send a letter with you to the king of Israel."

So Naaman went and took with him gifts of silver and gold and clothing. He gave the letter to the king of Israel. It read: I have sent my servant Naaman to you to cure him of his skin disease.

When the king of Israel read the letter, he tore his clothes and asked, "Am I God? Does this man expect me to cure him? He's only picking a fight with me!"

When Elisha heard that the king had torn his clothes, he sent him a message, "Why have you torn your clothes? Send Naaman to me, and he will know there is a prophet in Israel." So Naaman came and stood at the door of Elisha's house.

Elisha sent him a messenger, who said, "Go wash 7 times in the Jordan River, and you will be healed."

But Naaman got angry. He said, "I thought he would come out and call on the name of Yahweh. I thought he would wave his hand over me and heal me. Aren't the rivers of Damascus (duh MAS kuhs) better than the waters of Israel? Couldn't I wash in them and be clean?" So he turned and left in a rage.

But his servants said, "If the prophet had told you to do some great thing, wouldn't you have done it? Why not do this simple thing?"

So Naaman went and dipped himself in the Jordan 7 times, as Elisha had told him. His skin was healed! Naaman went back to Elisha and said, "There's no God in the whole world except in Israel. Please accept a gift from your servant."

But Elisha said, "I will not accept a gift."

Naaman answered, "Then please let me take as much soil as a pair of mules can carry. For I will no longer make an offering to any other god but Yahweh.

So Elisha said, "Go in peace."

**Christ Connection:** Naaman was sick with a skin problem. His disease went away when he washed in the river. All people are sick with a sin problem. They need a Healer. When we trust Jesus as Lord and Savior, God forgives our sin and heals us.

**Big Picture Question:** Who heals us from our sin?

**Big Picture Answer:** Jesus heals us from our sin.

Hoshea (hoh SHEE uh), the son of Elah, became king over Israel. He ruled from the city of Samaria and was king for 9 years. Hoshea did what was evil in the Lord's sight, but he was not as bad as the kings who had come before him.

While Hoshea was king, Israel was attacked by the king of Assyria (uh SIHR ee uh) and was forced to pay him money to keep the Israelites safe. But then Hoshea stopped paying the money, and he plotted with the Pharaoh of Egypt against the king of Assyria. The king found out and threw Hoshea in prison. Then the king of Assyria invaded the whole land of Israel. His army marched up to Samaria and held it for three years. Many Israelites were captured and sent back to Assyria.

Now this disaster happened because the people of Israel had sinned against God by worshipping false gods. God warned the people not to worship idols. He sent messages to them from every prophet, saying, "Turn from your evil ways and keep My commands."

But the people were stubborn, and they would not listen. They rejected God and His words and His promises. They chased after worthless idols and became worthless themselves. They made images of calves to worship. They worshipped the stars, and they served Baal. They devoted themselves to doing what was evil in the Lord's sight.

Because of this, the Lord was very angry with Israel. This was the reason God allowed them to be captured and taken from the land He had given them. Only the tribe of Judah remained. But even Judah did not keep God's commands—they also worshipped false gods. So God rejected all the descendants of Israel, and He handed them over to their enemies. In this way, the people were scattered from the land God had given them.

**Christ Connection:** When the Israelites disobeyed God, God judged their sin and punished them by removing them from His presence. Jesus took the punishment for our sin upon Himself in order to unite and restore us, bring us into God's presence, and keep us there.

**Big Picture Question:** Why did God scatter His people?

**Big Picture Answer:** God's people sinned against Him by worshipping false gods.

The people of Israel turned away from God and worshipped false gods. They treated their fellow Israelites terribly. They cheated the poor and made them slaves.

Now, Amos was a shepherd who lived during the days of King Uzziah (uh ZI uh) of Judah and King Jeroboam (jer uh BOH uhm) of Israel. God called him to be a prophet. He sent Amos to warn the people that they would be punished if they didn't turn back to the Lord.

God told Amos to say, "The people don't do what is right. So the Lord God says, 'An enemy will surround the land. He will destroy your fortresses and plunder your cities."

Then God showed Amos 5 visions. In the first vision, Amos saw a swarm of locusts that ate all the plants of the land. Amos begged with God not to do this. So God said, "It will not happen."

In the second vision, God showed Amos a judgment by fire. The fire destroyed the land. Again, Amos begged God not to do this. So God said, "This will not happen either."

In the third vision, God showed Amos a plumb line. Then the Lord said, "I am setting a plumb line among My people Israel. I will judge them, and I will no longer spare them."

In the fourth vision, the Lord God showed Amos a basket of summer fruit. Then God said, "I will no longer spare My people Israel. There will be a terrible earthquake and the sun will go down at noon. Hear this! I will send a famine through the land. It will not be a famine of bread or water, but of hearing the words of the Lord. People will search from sea to sea, looking for the word of the Lord, but they will not find it."

In the fifth vision, God said, "I will destroy this sinful kingdom from the face of the earth. But I will not totally destroy the house of Jacob. All the sinners among My people will die by the sword. But I will rebuild the fallen house of David. I will restore the fortunes of My people Israel. They will never again be uprooted from the land I have given them. Yahweh your God has spoken."

**Christ Connection:** Amos predicted that because of their sin, Israel would experience a time when God would not speak to them. Israel would search for God, but they would not find Him. Israel's spiritual famine ended when God sent Jesus into the world. Jesus came to tell people what God is like and to provide salvation to all kinds of people.

**Big Picture Question:** How does God feel when we are unfair to people?

**Big Picture Answer:** God is angry when people are treated badly.

# Hosea, Prophet to Israel

Hosea was a prophet of God during the times of King Uzziah (uh ZI uh), King Jotham, King Ahaz, and King Hezekiah (hez uh KI uh) of Judah, and of King Jeroboam (jer uh BOH uhm) of Israel. At this time, Israel turned her back on God and chased after other gods. The Lord God was very angry, and He declared that He would punish Israel for her unfaithfulness.

When the Lord first spoke to Hosea, He said: "Go and marry an unfaithful wife and have children. She will be like Israel who has abandoned Me and been unfaithful to Me."

So Hosea married Gomer, and they had children. God told Hosea what to name the children. Their names were warnings to the people of Israel. The first son was named Jezreel, because God said He would put an end to the kingdom of Israel at the city of Jezreel.

The second child was a girl, and God said, "Name her No Compassion, for I will no longer have compassion on the house of Israel.

Next came a son, and the Lord said: "Name him Not My People, for you are not My people, and I will not be your God."

Israel had sinned against God, and He was going to punish them. But even with all their sins, God did not stop loving His people. Yes, He would punish them, but the punishment was to make Israel see her sins and turn back to God. Then He would bless her again.

So Hosea called for the people to repent and to turn back to God: "Israel, return to Yahweh your God, for you have stumbled in your sin. Return to the Lord and say 'Forgive all our sins.'"

God promised that He would forgive the Israelites when they returned to Him. He would have compassion on His people. And He would say "You are My people," and they will say, "You are My God."

Hosea reminded the people that, "the ways of the Lord are right, and the righteous walk in them, but the rebellious stumble in them."

**Christ Connection:** Hosea's relationship with Gomer reminds us of God's relationship with the people of Israel and with us. Even though God's people are unfaithful and love other things more than they love God, God still loves us. It was because of His love that God sent Jesus to die on the cross for our sin and bring us back to Him.

**Big Picture Question:** How does Hosea remind us of God?

**Big Picture Answer:** God loves us even when we are unfaithful.

# Jonah, Prophet to Nineveh

One day, God told His prophet Jonah to go to the city of Nineveh (NIN uh vuh) and give them a warning. But the people of Nineveh were very wicked, and Jonah didn't want to go there. So he ran away to a ship headed for Tarshish (TAHR shish). So God sent a terrible storm against the ship. The sailors were terrified, and each cried out to his own god. Meanwhile, Jonah was asleep inside the ship!

The captain woke him with a shout, "Why are you sleeping? Call to your god. Maybe your god will save us."

The sailors then cast lots to see who was to blame for the storm—it was Jonah. "What have you done?" they asked. "How do we calm this sea?"

"You must throw me overboard," Jonah said.

"No!" the sailors cried. But the storm got worse and worse—until they threw Jonah into the sea. Then . . . the storm stopped.

God sent a huge fish to swallow Jonah. For 3 days and 3 nights, Jonah was inside the fish! Jonah prayed to God, and the fish spit Jonah onto dry land. Once again, God told Jonah to go to Nineveh. This time, Jonah went!

Jonah walked through Nineveh preaching, "In 40 days, Nineveh will be destroyed!"

When the king of Nineveh heard this, he sent an order to all his people: "Everyone must pray to God and turn from his evil ways. Then maybe God will not destroy us!"

When God saw that the people were sorry, he didn't destroy them. But Jonah was furious. "That's why I didn't want to come here!" he said to God. "I know You are slow to get angry and rich in love. Just take my life—it's better for me to die than to live."

Then Jonah left the city and sat down to see what would happen. God made a plant grow up to give Jonah shade. Jonah was very pleased with the plant. But the next day, God sent a worm to attack the plant, and it died. The sun beat down on Jonah's head until he said again, "It's better for me to die!"

God asked, "Is it right for you to be angry about the plant?"

"Yes, it is" said Jonah stubbornly.

God said, "You cared about the plant, which you didn't make grow. So shouldn't I care about the people of Nineveh?"

**Christ Connection:** God displayed His mercy and grace by forgiving the people of Nineveh when they repented of their sin. God would show His love to the rest of the world by sending His Son, Jesus, to die on the cross. God saves those who trust in Jesus and repent of their sin.

**Big Picture Question:** How can we be forgiven?

**Big Picture Answer:** God forgives people when they are sorry and ask for forgiveness.

The people of Judah had been attacked by locusts. Not just one or two locusts—or even a few hundred or thousand—but great clouds and swarms of them. Like a terrible army, the locusts marched across the land, destroying everything. They ate all the crops in the fields and even stripped the bark off the trees!

After the locusts, there came a terrible drought. The land dried up. The grapevines withered, and all the trees in the orchards—fig, apple, and pomegranate—shriveled up. There was no food, and the land was filled with sadness.

The people of Judah still did not follow God with all their hearts. So God came to the prophet Joel and gave him a message for His people:

"Let all the people of the land tremble, for the Day of the Lord is coming. A great army of people is coming. They are coming for war."

God was warning His people that a great army was coming against them. He was going to let that army attack His people as punishment for their sins. The soldiers of that army would be like the locusts—too many to count and destroying everything in their path.

Joel warned the people to turn back to God. "Cry out to God. Tear your hearts, not just your clothes," he said. "Return to the Lord your God. He is compassionate, slow to anger, and rich in love. If you turn back to Him, maybe He will save you from this army and bless you instead."

Then God made a promise to His people: If they would turn back to Him, then He would protect them. He would drive away their enemies and bless His people. When that happened, God said, "You will know that I am Yahweh your God."

**Christ Connection:** God used locusts and drought to get Judah's attention. They had turned from God, and the prophet Joel called them to repent. Like Joel, Jesus calls sinners to repent. Jesus died and was resurrected so all nations could experience repentance and forgiveness (Luke 24:46–47).

**Big Picture Question:** What does God want for all people?

**Big Picture Answer:** God wants all people to turn to Him and be saved.

# God Called Isaiah

In the year that King Uzziah (uh ZI uh) of Judah died, Isaiah had a vision. In this vision, he was called to be a prophet of God. Isaiah saw the Lord seated on His throne in heaven, and God's robe filled the temple. Seraphim (SER uh fim), which are heavenly beings, stood above the Lord. Each one had 6 wings: with 2 he covered his face, with 2 he covered his feet, and with 2 he flew. The seraphim said,

Holy, holy, holy is the Lord of Hosts;

His glory fills the whole earth.

Then Isaiah said: "Woe is me! I am ruined because I am a man of unclean lips, and I live among a people of unclean lips, and because my eyes have seen the King, the Lord of Hosts."

Then one of the seraphim flew over to Isaiah. In his hand was a glowing coal that he had taken from the altar. He touched Isaiah's mouth with it and said: "Now that this has touched your lips, your wickedness is removed and your sin is made right."

Then Isaiah heard the voice of the Lord, saying, "Who should I send? Who will go for Us?"

And Isaiah said: "Here I am. Send me."

So God told Isaiah to go to the people and warn them to turn back to God. If they would turn back, their land would be healed. But God also told Isaiah that the people would not listen to him, and they would not turn back to God.

Isaiah asked how long he had to preach this message. God answered, "Until the cities lie in ruins and the houses are without people. Until the Lord drives the people far away, leaving the land empty. But even then some will remain in the land. Some will survive, and they will be My people again."

**Christ Connection:** Before Jesus came to the earth as a man, He lived forever in heaven. Jesus wanted someone to go and warn His people to stop sinning and turn back to Him. Jesus called Isaiah to be that person. But before Isaiah could serve God as a prophet, Jesus needed to take away his sin. Today, Jesus takes away our sins when we believe in Him so that we can be His servants.

**Big Picture Question:** How could Isaiah stand before God?

**Big Picture Answer:** Isaiah could stand before God because God took away Isaiah's sin.

# Isaiah Confronted King Ahaz

Isaiah was a prophet of God during the time that King Ahaz was ruler of Judah.

Now at that time, King Rezin (REE zin) of Aram and King Pekah (PEE kah) of Israel waged war against the city of Jerusalem in Judah. They could not capture it, though. But when King Ahaz heard that the armies of Aram were nearby, he and his people began to tremble with fear—like trees of a forest shaking in the wind. King Ahaz began to think about asking the king of Assyria to help protect him and the people of Judah.

So the Lord said to Isaiah, "Go and meet Ahaz. Say to him: Calm down. Don't be afraid because of King Rezin and King Pekah. Yes, they have plotted against you. They want to capture Judah and take your throne. But if you will trust in Me, I won't let that happen. If you don't trust in Me, you will fall."

God wanted King Ahaz to trust in His power to save him, rather than trusting in the king of Assyria. So the Lord spoke again to King Ahaz: "Ask Me for a sign."

But Ahaz said, "I will not ask for a sign. I will not test the Lord."

Isaiah said, "Listen! Will you test the patience of God? The Lord Himself will give you a sign: The virgin will have a son, and name him Immanuel. But before the boy is old enough to reject what is bad and choose what is good, the two kings you fear will be destroyed. Then the king of Assyria will come after you and your kingdom. The land will be destroyed with famine and wars."

These things would happen because King Ahaz and his people didn't choose to trust in God. Isaiah's words were for right then, but they were also for a future time—the time when Jesus would come. For Jesus would be born of a virgin and He would be named *Immanuel*, which means, "God with us."

**Christ Connection:** Through the prophet Isaiah, God promised to send Immanuel, which means "God with us." Jesus fulfilled this promise when He came to earth and was born of a virgin. Jesus is our Immanuel, God with us.

**Big Picture Question:** What does *Immanuel* mean?

**Big Picture Answer:** God is with us.

# Hezekiah, Judah's Faithful King

Hezekiah (hez uh KI uh) became king of Judah when he was 25 years old. He ruled in Jerusalem for 29 years. Hezekiah did what was right in the Lord's sight, just as King David had done. He removed the places where the false gods were worshipped and shattered their sacred poles. Hezekiah trusted God and followed the laws the Lord had given to Moses.

Now, in the fourteenth year of King Hezekiah, the king of Assyria attacked the cities of Judah and captured them. Then the king of Assyria (uh SIRH ee uh) sent his officials, along with a massive army, to Jerusalem. The officials called out to the people of Jerusalem: "Don't let Hezekiah trick you! He can't save you. Don't let him talk you into trusting the Lord."

When King Hezekiah heard what the Assyrians said, he tore his clothes and covered himself with sackcloth. Then he sent messengers to the prophet Isaiah, asking him to pray for God's people.

Isaiah sent a message back to Hezekiah: "The Lord says: 'Don't be afraid because of what these people have said against Me. The king of Assyria will go back to his own land. And he will die there by the sword.'"

Hezekiah then went up to the Lord's temple and prayed: "Lord God of Israel, please save us from the king of Assyria so that all the world will know that You alone are God."

God heard Hezekiah's prayer. That night the angel of the Lord struck down 185,000 men in the camp of the Assyrians. When the people got up the next morning—they found all the dead bodies! So the king of Assyria left and went back home—where he was killed by two of his own sons!

A little while later, Hezekiah became very sick. Isaiah even came and told him that God had said he would die. Hezekiah turned his face to the wall and prayed, "Please Lord, remember how I have served You faithfully."

Isaiah hadn't even left the courtyard yet when God said, "Go back to Hezekiah and tell him I have heard his prayer. I will heal him and add 15 years to his life."

Hezekiah asked Isaiah for a sign that he truly would get better. So Isaiah called out to God, and God moved the shadow backward up the stairway by 10 steps! Then Hezekiah was healed.

**Christ Connection:** Hezekiah was a faithful king who led the people of Judah to worship God like they were supposed to worship. Like Hezekiah, Jesus is our faithful King who will one day return to rule over the earth and make all things the way they are supposed to be.

**Big Picture Question:** Whose prayers does God hear?

**Big Picture Answer:** God hears the prayers of His people because they trust in Him.

Isaiah was a prophet of God. God gave him messages to share with His people. Sometimes they were messages about how the people needed to change their ways. But sometimes, God's messages were about the coming of One who would save the people. This message was about Jesus—and God gave it to Isaiah 700 hundred years before Jesus was born!

Isaiah preached that Jesus would be hated and would suffer:

*He was despised and rejected by men, a man of suffering who knew what sickness was.*

*He was like someone people turned away from; He was despised, and we didn't value Him.*

Isaiah told about how Jesus would suffer for our sins and how His suffering would save us:

*But He was pierced because of our transgressions . . . and we are healed by His wounds.*

The people would wander away from God like sheep, Isaiah said. They would do what they wanted, but God would punish Jesus for their sins:

*We all went astray like sheep; we all have turned to our own way; and the LORD has punished Him for the iniquity of us all.*

Jesus would not argue with those who wanted to kill him:

*Like a lamb led to the slaughter and like a sheep silent before her shearers, He did not open His mouth.*

Even though He was innocent, Jesus would die like a criminal and be buried in a rich man's tomb:

*They made His grave with the wicked and with a rich man at His death, although He had done no violence and had not spoken deceitfully.*

Jesus would allow all this to happen to Him, so that we might live with Him in heaven one day:

*He submitted Himself to death, and was counted among the rebels; yet He bore the sin of many and interceded for the rebels.*

All of these things came true—just as God told Isaiah they would. Jesus was hated. He let Himself be killed on a cross like a criminal. He was buried in the tomb of a rich man named Joseph of Arimathea. And because He took the punishment for our sins on Himself, those who follow Him are forgiven.

**Christ Connection:** God decided a very long time ago that Jesus would die on the cross for our sins. Seven hundred years before Jesus was born, the prophet Isaiah wrote that this would happen! Jesus was the servant who suffered so that those who put their faith in Him could be healed of their sins.

**Big Picture Question:** Why did Jesus have to suffer?

**Big Picture Answer:** Jesus had to suffer so that we could be healed of our sins.

# Micah, Prophet to Judah

Micah (MI kuh) was a prophet of God sent to the people of Judah. He lived during the time of kings Jotham (JO thuhm), Ahaz, and Hezekiah (hez uh KI uh). At that time, both Israel and Judah had become very wealthy, but they had also become full of sin. The leaders took bribes, the rich cheated the poor, and even the priests didn't teach the people God's true words. The people ignored God's laws and worshipped idols.

So God sent Micah to warn the people. Micah said to them: "Listen, all you peoples. Pay attention! The Lord has seen your sins. He is leaving His holy temple and coming down to trample the heights of the earth. The mountains will melt beneath Him, and the valleys will split apart. All this will happen because of your sins."

To those who cheated the poor, Micah said: "Woe to those who dream up wickedness! They take away a man's house and inheritance. The Lord says, 'I am planning a disaster against this nation. Then you will not walk so proudly because you will be ruined.'"

To the rulers, false prophets, and even priests who cheated and abused God's people, this is what he said, "Now listen, you rulers. You should know what is right, but you hate good and love evil." Micah warned that a time would come when these leaders would cry out to God for help, but He would not listen because of their crimes.

Micah told the people why God was angry. When God had saved His people from Egypt and from slavery, He had told them "to act justly, to love faithfulness, and to walk humbly with your God." But the people didn't do that! So God would let them be attacked and taken captive to Babylon because of their sins.

Micah gave many warnings, but he also gave the people hope. He said that God would rescue them from Babylon—and He already had a plan!

Then Micah gave them the greatest hope of all—the hope of a Savior: "Now, Bethlehem Ephrathah (EF ruh thuh), you are small among the clans of Judah. But One will come from you to be ruler over Israel for Me. He will shepherd My people in the name of Yahweh. His greatness will extend to the ends of the earth. He will be their peace." Micah was speaking about Jesus!

**Christ Connection:** God demanded righteousness from His people, but they forgot about God and faced slavery. The prophet Micah gave the people a message of hope: a leader was coming who would free God's people. He would be a shepherd and a king. The righteous ruler promised by Micah is the Lord Jesus Christ.

**Big Picture Question:** What does God want us to do?

**Big Picture Answer:** God wants us to obey Him because we love Him.

Josiah (jo-SIGH-uh) was only 8 years old when he became king of Judah. He ruled for 31 years in Jerusalem. While he was still young, Josiah began to seek God—unlike the other kings before him. Josiah shattered all the idols and carved images in Judah and Jerusalem. He even went all throughout Israel, destroying the altars to Baal and the carved images of false gods.

In his eighteenth year as king, Josiah sent his officials to repair the temple of God. Money had been collected from the people to help with the repairs. So the officials took the money to Hilkiah (hil KI uh), the high priest. He used it to pay the carpenters and builders and to buy stone and timbers.

When Hilkiah was bringing the money out of the temple, he found the book of the God's laws written by Moses. Hilkiah gave it to Shaphan (SHAY fuhn), the king's secretary. He took the book to King Josiah and read it to the king.

When the king heard the words of the law, he tore his clothes. His people had not been obeying all of God's laws. Then he ordered Hilkiah, and others to go. "Ask Yahweh about the words of this book," he said. "For great is the Lord's wrath that will be poured out on us because our fathers didn't keep word of the Lord."

So Hilkiah and the others went to the prophetess Huldah (HUL duh), who lived in Jerusalem. She told them, "This is what Yahweh says: 'I am about to bring disaster on this place and on its people, because they have abandoned Me and worshipped other gods.' But say this to King Josiah, 'Because your heart was tender, and because you tore your clothes and wept before Me when you heard My words, you will go to your grave in peace. Your eyes will not see all the disaster that I am bringing on this place and its people.'"

Hilkiah reported all this to the king. So Josiah gathered all the people, from great to small. He read to them all the words of the book of law that had been found in the Lord's temple. Then King Josiah promised to follow the Lord and to keep His commands with all his heart. The people of Jerusalem promised to do the same. And throughout the rule of King Josiah, the people did not turn aside from following Yahweh, the God of their fathers.

**Christ Connection:** Josiah had great respect for God's law. He allowed God's Word to control what he did as a king. Josiah wanted God's people to love God and obey the law too. When Jesus came to the earth, He respected the law, loved it, and fulfilled the law by obeying it perfectly.

**Big Picture Question:** How did Josiah help the Israelites?

**Big Picture Answer:** Josiah led the Israelites to obey the Word of God.

Zephaniah (zef uh NI ah) was a prophet of God. God told him about the coming Day of the Lord—the day when God would judge the world for all its sins. God said, "On that day, I will completely sweep away everything from the face of the earth. I will sweep away man and animal. I will sweep away the birds of the sky and the fish of the sea. I will cut off mankind from the face of the earth."

Zephaniah urged the people to return to God before it was too late. "Gather yourselves together," he said, "before the day of the Lord's anger overtakes you. Seek the Lord and obey His laws. Try to do what is right and to be humble. Then perhaps you will be hidden from His anger."

There would be a day of terrible judgment coming to those who didn't obey God, but there would also be a great day coming for those who did put their trust in Him.

For God said, "I will remove the proud and arrogant people from among you. I will leave a meek and humble people, and they will take refuge in the name of Yahweh. At that time, I will give you fame and praise among all the peoples of the earth. I will restore your fortunes before your eyes."

In that day, Zephaniah said that the people would "sing for joy and shout loudly!" God would take away their punishment. He would defeat their enemies, because God is a warrior who saves His people. God will rejoice over His people with gladness, and quiet them with His love. The Lord will delight in His people with shouts of joy.

**Christ Connection:** Zephaniah prophesied about the Day of the Lord, when God will judge the world for its sin and Jesus Christ will return. Zephaniah also described another day when Christ will restore all things to the way they are supposed to be.

**Big Picture Question:** What will happen on the Day of the Lord?

**Big Picture Answer:** God will judge the sinners and save those who trust in Jesus.

Habakkuk (huh BAK uhk) was a prophet of God. But unlike other prophets who spoke to the people for God, Habakkuk spoke to God for the people. As Habakkuk looked at the world around him, it seemed that evil was everywhere. So he turned to God for answers and help.

Habakkuk prayed:

*"How long, Lord, must I call for help? Why do You put up with all this wrongdoing? There is violence right in front of me. There is no justice."*

Then God told Habakkuk how he was going to punish the people for their wickedness. He was going to let them be taken by their enemies to Babylon. God said,

*"Look! I am raising up the armies of Babylon. They are fierce and terrifying. Their horses are swifter than leopards and more fierce than wolves. Their horsemen fly like an eagle, swooping to devour. They gather prisoners like sand. They mock kings, and laugh at every fortress. Strength is their god."*

Habakkuk prayed again, saying,

*"Lord, You raised them up to punish us. But they are even more wicked than we are! Why do you let them swallow us up?"*

God said, "The enemy is certainly coming, but the righteous one will live by his faith." This meant that God's people must trust in Him, even during hard times.

So Habakkuk prayed a third time:

*"Lord, I stand in awe of Your deeds. You split the earth with rivers. The mountains see You and shudder. The deep roars and lifts its waves high. Sun and moon stand still in their places, at the flash of Your flying arrows, at the brightness of Your shining spear. You come out to save Your people. You crush the leader of the house of the wicked.*

*"Now I must quietly wait for the day of trouble to come against the people invading us. Though there is no fruit on the vines, and the fields produce no food, though there are no sheep in the pen and no cattle in the stalls, yet I will rejoice in the God of my salvation! Yahweh is my strength!"*

**Christ Connection:** Habakkuk lived at a time when evil seemed to be everywhere. By faith, he trusted God's promise that God would deliver His people. Injustice, violence, and wickedness surround us today, but we can live by faith and trust that Jesus will return to make all things right.

**Big Picture Question:** How do God's people live in bad times?

**Big Picture Answer:** God's people trust God to take care of them.

Nineveh (NIN uh vuh) was the capital city of Assyria (uh SIHR ee uh), the enemy of God's people. Many years before, God sent the prophet Jonah to warn the city of Nineveh to change its evil ways—and they did. So God didn't destroy them.

But now, Nineveh was more evil than ever before. They attacked God's people and were cruel to them. So God sent the prophet Nahum (NAY huhm) to tell His people that Nineveh would be defeated. While this was bad news for Nineveh, it was a great comfort to the people of Judah. Nahum's name even means "comfort."

This is the message that God gave Nahum:

The Lord takes revenge against His foes. He is furious with His enemies. Though He is slow to anger, He is great in power. The Lord will never leave the guilty unpunished.

The mountains quake before Him, and the hills melt. The earth trembles at His presence. No one can stand against the Lord's anger. Even rocks are shattered before Him.

The Lord is good. He cares for those who take shelter in Him. But He will completely destroy Nineveh. They are strong and many in number, but they will still be mowed down.

Because the Israelites had sinned against God by worshipping false gods, He had allowed Nineveh to attack His people as punishment for their sins. But the time of their punishment was over. God said, "I will punish you no longer. I will rescue you."

To the people of Nineveh, God said, "There will be no children to carry on your name. I will destroy the carved idols and images of your gods. I will prepare your grave. But I will restore the majesty of Israel and of Jacob."

"Beware," God warned Nineveh. "I am against you. I will make your chariots go up in smoke. Your people will be across the mountains. There will be no healing for your wounds. All who hear the news about you will clap their hands, for who has not experienced your constant cruelty?"

**Christ Connection:** Nahum brought a message of comfort to God's people, reminding them that God loves His people and will protect them from their enemies. Jesus also brought a message of comfort to His people. Jesus assured us of salvation and peace. All of the enemies of God and the enemies of God's children were defeated at the cross. In the end, all evil will be finally punished.

**Big Picture Question:** Why did God destroy Nineveh?

**Big Picture Answer:** The people of Nineveh didn't love God or His people.

# God Called Jeremiah

Jeremiah was a priest of God in Judah during the days of King Josiah (joh SI uh), King Jehoiakim (juh HOI uh kim), and King Zedekiah (zed uh KI ah), when the people of Jerusalem went into exile.

God called Jeremiah to be His prophet. God said to him: "I chose you before I formed you in the womb. I set you apart before you were born. I appointed you a prophet to the nations."

But Jeremiah said, "Oh no, Lord God! Look, I don't know how to speak since I am only a youth."

Then the Lord said to Jeremiah: "Don't say, 'I am only a youth,' for you will go to everyone I send you to and speak whatever I tell you. Don't be afraid of anyone, for I will be with you to save you."

Then the Lord reached out His hand, touched Jeremiah's mouth, and said: "I have now filled your mouth with My words."

God showed Jeremiah 2 visions to show him what was coming. After Jeremiah saw the first vision, God asked, "What do you see, Jeremiah?"

Jeremiah said, "I see the branch of an almond tree."

God said, "Yes, for I am watching My word to see that it is fulfilled." God meant that just as an almond tree blooms in the spring, God would cause Jeremiah to bloom with fruitful words from Him.

Then God asked again, "What do you see?"

And Jeremiah answered, "I see a boiling pot. It is tilted from the north to the south."

Then the Lord said to Jeremiah, "This means that disaster will be poured out from the north on all who live in the land." The Lord was telling Jeremiah that armies would come from the north and attack Judah. This would happen to punish Judah for worshipping false gods and idols that they made with their own hands.

Then God said to Jeremiah, "Now, get ready. Stand up and tell the people everything that I command you. Don't be afraid of them. I will make you like a fortified city against the kings of Judah, its officials, its priests, and the population. They will fight against you but never defeat you, because I am with you and I will rescue you."

**Christ Connection:** God called Jeremiah to be a prophet to the nations. Jeremiah challenged the way people lived in Judah and led them to turn away from their idol worship and other sins. Christ did more than challenge how people lived; He called all men to turn from their sins, and He provided the way for people to have a relationship with God.

**Big Picture Question:** Why did God call Jeremiah?

**Big Picture Answer:** God called Jeremiah to be a prophet. He chose Jeremiah before he was born.

Jeremiah was a prophet of God during the rule of King Jehoiakim (juh HOI uh kim) of Judah. God said to Jeremiah: "Take a scroll, and write on it all the words I have spoken to you. Perhaps if the people hear about all the disasters I am planning to bring on them, they will turn from their evil ways. Then I will forgive their sins."

So Jeremiah called for Baruch (BAY ruhk), his scribe, and had him write on a scroll all the words the Lord had spoken to him. Then Jeremiah said, "Go to the temple and read the scroll to the people. Perhaps they will turn from their evil ways."

So Baruch went the Lord's temple and read the scroll to all the people. One man heard him and went to tell the king's officials. The officials sent for Baruch and asked him to read the scroll to them. When they heard the words of the Lord, they turned to each other in fear and said to Baruch, "We must tell the king all these things!"

But the officials were afraid of what the king might do to Baruch and Jeremiah, so they said, "Hide yourselves and tell no one where you are." Then the officials left the scroll in one of the chambers and went to tell the king what the Lord had said.

The king sent for the scroll and ordered that it be read to him. But the king and his servants were not frightened by the words of God. In fact, as soon as part of the scroll was read, King Jehoiakim would cut that part off with a knife and throw it into the fire! He did this until the entire scroll was burned! Then the king ordered that Baruch and Jeremiah be arrested, but the Lord had hidden them.

But God would not allow His words to be destroyed so easily. So God said to Jeremiah: "Take another scroll, and write on it all the words that were on the first scroll." Then God said, "I will punish King Jehoiakim, his descendants, and his officers. And I will bring on the people of Judah all the disasters that I warned them about."

**Christ Connection:** Jeremiah dictated the message of God to be written on a scroll for the people so they would know that God was displeased, that they needed to stop sinning, and that they should turn back to God. Christ brought the same message. He was called "the Word" (John 1:14) and came to live among the people, explain their need to turn back to God, and sacrifice His life to make a way for people to turn from sin and to know and love God.

**Big Picture Question:** Why did Jeremiah warn God's people?

**Big Picture Answer:** God wanted His people to know they were in danger, to stop sinning, and to turn back to Him.

# Judah Was Taken into Captivity

The people of Judah made Jehoahaz (juh HOH uh haz) king in place of his father, Josiah. Jehoahaz was 23 years old when he became king. He ruled for 3 months in Jerusalem. The king of Egypt took his throne and made his brother Jehoiakim (juh HOI uh kim) king over Judah and Jerusalem.

Jehoiakim was 25 years old when he became king, and he ruled for 11 years in Jerusalem. He worshipped idols and did what was evil in the sight of God. King Nebuchadnezzar (neb uh kuhd NEZ uhr) of Babylon attacked and captured him. He put Jehoiakim in shackles and took him to Babylon Nebuchadnezzar also took some things from the Lord's temple and put them in his temple in Babylon. Jehoiakim's son Jehoiachin (juh HOI uh kin) became king in his place.

Jehoiachin was 18 years old when he became king. He ruled for 3 months and 10 days in Jerusalem. He also did what was evil in the Lord's sight. In the spring Nebuchadnezzar sent for him and brought him to Babylon along with more valuable things from the Lord's temple. Then he made Jehoiachin's brother Zedekiah (zed uh KI uh) king over Judah and Jerusalem.

Zedekiah was 21 years old when he became king, and he ruled for 11 years. He, too, did evil in the sight of God. Zedekiah was stubborn and hardened his heart against God. He not only did was evil in the sight of God, but he also lead the people in worshipping idols. Then King Zedekiah rebelled against King Nebuchadnezzar.

Now, for many years, God sent prophets to warn His people to turn from their evil ways and to stop worshipping idols. But the people scoffed at God's prophets and hated His words. The Lord's anger was so stirred up against His people that there was no remedy. So He raised up the king of Babylon and handed his people over to him to be punished. The king took everything to Babylon—all the treasures of the Lord's temple and all the treasures of the king. Then they burned God's temple, tore down Jerusalem's wall, burned down all its palaces, and destroyed all its valuable articles. Those who were not killed were taken to Babylon to be servants of the king. All this happened to fulfill the words that the Lord spoke to His prophet Jeremiah.

**Christ Connection:** God righteously punished His people for their sin but remained faithful to them, keeping the promise He made to David to provide a king. Ultimately, God punished our sin through His Son Jesus and made Him our forever King.

**Big Picture Question:** How did God punish His people for their sin?

**Big Picture Answer:** God allowed their enemies to capture them and to destroy Jerusalem.

Ezekiel (ih ZEE kee uhl) was a prophet of God. At that time, God's people were sinning against Him in terrible ways. They not only worshipped false gods and idols, but they even worshipped them in God's own temple! The day was coming when God would judge the people for their sins.

One day, God showed Ezekiel a vision. In the vision, Ezekiel saw cherubim (CHER uh bim), which are angelic beings. Above their heads, there was something like a throne made of sapphire stone. The Lord spoke to a man dressed in linen and said, "Go and fill your hands with hot coals from beneath the cherubim and scatter them over the city." As Ezekiel watched, a cherub reached out his hand to the fire and took some coals. Then he put them into the hands of the man dressed in linen, who took them and went out. This was to show that God would soon be judging His people for their sins.

Now at that time, the glory of the Lord lived in the temple in a cloud. And in his vision, Ezekiel saw the temple filled with the cloud. This showed the people that the Lord was with them.

Beside the cherubim were 4 wheels. Each of the wheels was made the same—like a wheel within a wheel. The wheels were full of eyes all around and were called "the wheel-work." Each wheel had 4 faces: the face of a cherub, a man, a lion, and an eagle. When the cherubim moved, the wheels moved with them.

Then Ezekiel saw the cloud, which was the glory of the Lord move away from the threshold of the temple. The cherubim also lifted their wings and rose from the earth, with the wheels beside them as they went. The glory of the Lord rose above them, and it stood at the eastern gate of the Lord's house. This was to show that God had decided to leave His temple. Since His people no longer followed Him, He would no longer live among them.

**Christ Connection:** God left the temple because He was unhappy with His peoples' sin. Sin separates people from God. Jesus came to earth to fix our relationship with God by taking the punishment of our sin for us. Because of Christ, we can enjoy God's presence.

**Big Picture Question:** How did God show He was unhappy with Israel?

**Big Picture Answer:** God's presence left the temple.

At this time, the people of Israel were divided into 2 kingdoms: Israel and Judah. But they had both been attacked by the Babylonians and were scattered from their nation. The Lord, however, had a plan to save His people.

One day, the Lord picked up the prophet Ezekiel and set him down in the middle of a valley. The valley was covered with bones, and they were very dry.

God asked Ezekiel, "Can these bones live?"

"Lord God, only You can know that," Ezekiel answered.

So God said, "Say to these bones: Dry bones, this is what the Lord says to you: I will make flesh grow on you and cover you with skin. I will put breath in you so that you come to life."

Ezekiel spoke to the bones as God said. While he was speaking, there was a great rattling sound. All around, the bones began to come together, bone by bone! As Ezekiel watched, flesh grew on them and skin covered them, but there was no breath in them.

Then God said, "Say this: Breath, come from the 4 winds and breathe into these bodies!" Ezekiel did as God said, and the breath entered them. They came to life and stood on their feet.

"These bones are like the people of Israel," God said. "They say, 'Our bones are dried up, and our hope is dead.' Go and say this to the people: The Lord says: I am going to raise you up and lead you into the land of Israel. I will put My Spirit in you, and you will live. Then you will know that I am Yahweh."

God also said: "Take a stick and write on it: Judah. Then take another stick and write on it: Israel. Hold them both together in your hand so that they become one stick. When the people ask what this means, tell them: This is what God says: I will gather the Israelites from all around. I will make them one nation again, with one king to rule them. They will no longer worship idols, and I will cleanse them from their sins. They will live in the land that I gave to Jacob. They will live in it forever with their children and grandchildren. My dwelling place will be with them. I will be their God, and they will be My people."

**Christ Connection:** God showed Ezekiel a valley of dry bones. The dry bones remind us what we are like when we sin. God had a plan for people who sin. Because Jesus came to earth, died, and was raised to life, He has the power to give us eternal life.

**Big Picture Question:** What plan did God show Ezekiel?

**Big Picture Answer:** God showed Ezekiel His plan to bring the Israelites back to their land and give them new life.

# Daniel and His Friends Obeyed God

In the time of King Jehoiakim (juh HOI uh kim) of Judah, the city of Jerusalem was captured by King Nebuchadnezzar (neb uh kuhd NEZ uhr) of Babylon. King Nebuchadnezzar ordered that some of the Israelites from the royal families and nobles be taken back to Babylon for training. They were to be good-looking, smart young men who would be able to serve in the king's palace. They would be trained for 3 years before being presented to the king. Daniel, Shadrach, Meshach, and Abednego were among the young men taken.

The king ordered that the young men be given food and wine from his own table. But it was against God's laws to eat the kinds of foods that the king ate. So Daniel asked the chief official if he could have other food. The chief official wanted to help Daniel, but he worried, "The king ordered that you be given this food and drink. If you start to look thinner than all the other young men, I'm afraid that the king might kill me."

So Daniel spoke to the guard who gave them their food, "Please test us for 10 days. Give us vegetables to eat and water to drink. Then see if we look healthy or not."

The guard agreed. At the end of 10 days, Daniel, Shadrach, Meshach, and Abednego looked better and healthier than all the other young men who were eating the king's food! So the guard agreed to keep giving them vegetables to eat and water to drink.

Because of their faithfulness, God gave these 4 young men great knowledge and understanding in every kind of literature and wisdom. Daniel also understood visions and dreams of every kind. At the end of their time of training, the 4 friends were presented to King Nebuchadnezzar. The king spoke with them, and he found that no one was as smart or understanding as Daniel, Shadrach, Meshach, and Abednego. So they began to serve in the king's court. And in everything they did, the king found that they were 10 times better than anyone else in his entire kingdom!

**Christ Connection:** Daniel, Shadrach, Meshach, and Abednego were taken to Babylon. They were ordered to eat food from the king's own table, but this was against God's laws. They chose to eat vegetables instead. Because they obeyed God—even in captivity—God blessed them with great wisdom and understanding.

**Big Picture Question:** What did Daniel and his friends do when they were captured?

**Big Picture Answer:** Daniel and his friends still obeyed God.

# Shadrach, Meshach, and Abednego

King Nebuchadnezzar (neb uh kuhd NEZ uhr) made a gold statue that was 90 feet high and 9 feet wide. Then he sent word to all his rulers and officials to come and see the statue. When everyone had gathered, one of the king's servants declared to all the people, "When you hear the sounds of music, you are to fall down and worship the gold statue. Whoever does not fall down and worship the statue will be thrown into a furnace of blazing fire."

So when the people heard the sounds of music, they fell down and worshipped the statue. Everyone, that is, except Shadrach, Meshach, and Abednego.

Some men went to the king and said, "Some Jews have ignored your orders. Shadrach, Meshach, and Abednego didn't fall down and worship the gold statue."

King Nebuchadnezzar was furious. He ordered that Shadrach, Meshach, and Abednego be brought to him. Then he asked, "Is it true that you didn't worship the statue? Now, when you hear the music, fall down and worship the statue. If you don't, you'll be thrown into the fire. What god can rescue you from my power?"

Shadrach, Meshach, and Abednego said, "The God we serve can rescue us from the fire, and He can rescue us from you. But even if He doesn't, we will not worship that gold statue."

This made Nebuchadnezzar even angrier! He ordered that the furnace be made seven times hotter than before. Then Shadrach, Meshach, and Abednego were tied up and carried to the furnace. The flames were so hot that they killed the men who carried them up! Then Shadrach, Meshach, and Abednego fell into the blazing fire.

Suddenly Nebuchadnezzar jumped up and shouted, "Didn't we throw 3 men into the fire?"

"Yes," said his officials.

"But look!" the king exclaimed. "I see 4 men walking around in the fire unharmed. And the fourth looks like a son of the gods!"

Nebuchadnezzar went to the furnace and called: "Servants of the Most High God—come out!" When Shadrach, Meshach, and Abednego came out, the king saw that the fire had not touched them. Not a hair on their heads was burned. They didn't even smell like smoke!

Nebuchadnezzar said, "Praise to the God of Shadrach, Meshach, and Abednego! He sent His angel to rescue His servants. No other god is able to deliver like this."

**Christ Connection:** Shadrach, Meshach, and Abednego were literally rescued from a fire. Christ came to save us from more than physical harm. Christ's sacrifice on the cross provided the way for us to be rescued from the punishment we deserve because of our sin and have eternal life.

**Big Picture Question:** Who protected Shadrach, Meshach, and Abednego?

**Big Picture Answer:** God protected them in the fire.

After King Nebuchadnezzar (neb uh kuhd NEZ uhr) died, Belshazzar (bel SHAZ uhr) became king. He held a great feast for 1,000 of his nobles. At the feast, Belshazzar sent for the gold and silver vessels that Nebuchadnezzar had taken from the Lord's temple in Jerusalem. Then the king and his guests drank wine from them and praised their false gods.

At that very moment, the fingers of a man's hand appeared and began writing on the wall of the king's palace! The king was so terrified that his face turned pale, his legs shook, and his knees knocked together. The king called for his wise men, and said, "Whoever reads this writing and tells me what it means will be clothed in purple, have a gold chain hung around his neck, and be made the third highest official in the kingdom." But no one could tell him what the writing meant.

Then the queen said to him, "Don't be terrified. There is a man who can explain this. Call for Daniel, and he'll tell you what this means."

So Daniel was brought before the king. The king offered Daniel the same rich rewards if he could tell him what the writing meant.

But Daniel said, "You may keep your gifts, but I will read this and tell you what it means. The Most High God gave power, greatness, and glory to Nebuchadnezzar. All peoples were terrified of him. But when he started to think he was better than God, his throne and his glory were taken from him. He was driven away from people and became like an animal. He lived with the wild donkeys and was fed grass like cattle until he confessed that God is ruler over all.

"But you, Belshazzar, have not humbled your heart. You have raised yourself up against the Lord of heaven. You have praised false gods and drunk wine from the Lord's vessels. So God sent this message to you:

*MENE, MENE, TEKEL, PARSIN.*

MENE (MEE nee) means that God has decided your kingdom will end.

TEKEL (TEE kel) means that you have been judged and found wanting.

PARSIN (PAHR sin) means that your kingdom has been divided and given to the Medes and Persians.

That very night Belshazzar was killed, and Darius the Mede became king in his place.

**Christ Connection:** God used Daniel's wisdom to get the king's attention about his idols. The king exalted himself by thinking he was better than God. God promised to humble the king. An idol is anything you love more than God, including yourself. Jesus came to destroy our idols and help us love God like we should.

**Big Picture Question:** What does God do to the proud?

**Big Picture Answer:** God humbles the proud.

Darius became king after Belshazzar (bel SHAZ uhr). He appointed 120 officials throughout his kingdom. Then he put 3 men in charge of those officials, and one of them was Daniel. Daniel was the best of them all, and King Darius planned to put him in charge of his whole kingdom. The other officials didn't like this and began to look for ways to get Daniel into trouble. But Daniel was trustworthy and honest. The men said, "We'll never find anything against Daniel unless it has something to do with his God."

So the officials went to King Darius and said, "You should make a law that says for 30 days no one may pray to any god or man except you. Anyone who breaks this law should be thrown into the lions' den." Darius like this idea. So he had the law written down, and he signed it. Now, once a law was signed, it could not be changed—not even by the king!

When Daniel heard about the law, he went into his house. He went to a window that faced Jerusalem and got down on his knees. Then he prayed to God, three times each day, just as he had always done.

The officials hurried to tell the king. "Daniel has ignored your law," they said. "He prays to His God." When Darius heard this, he was very upset, because he liked Daniel. All day, he tried to think of a way to save Daniel. But at sundown the officials said, "You know the law cannot be changed."

Darius had Daniel thrown into the lions' den. "May your God rescue you, Daniel!" he said. A large stone was rolled over the mouth of the den, and Darius sealed it with his ring. Then he went to his palace. He couldn't sleep and spent the whole night fasting.

At the first light of morning, Darius hurried to the lions' den. When he got there, he cried out, "Daniel, has your God been able to save you from the lions?"

Daniel said, "My God sent His angel and shut the lions' mouths. They haven't hurt me."

The king was overjoyed. Daniel was taken out of the den. And the men who had tried to trap Daniel were thrown in—they and all their families. Then King Darius wrote a new law: "All people must tremble in fear before the God of Daniel."

**Christ Connection:** God showed His power to rescue Daniel from the lions, but Daniel was just a small part of a much bigger story. God ultimately rescued us from a much bigger problem—sin and death—through the greatest hero of all, Jesus!

**Big Picture Question:** God rescued Daniel from death. What does God rescue us from?

**Big Picture Answer:** God rescues us from sin and death.

Obadiah (oh buh DI uh) was a prophet of the Lord. At that time, the land of Edom—a neighbor of Israel—was sinning against God. Now, the people of Edom came from the descendants of Esau, Jacob's brother. But they had turned away from the Lord God to worship false gods. Because they lived in the mountains, they trusted in those mountains, as well as their own strength and power to keep them safe. They didn't trust in God. The people were full of pride and thought that they were better than the other peoples around them.

So God gave Obadiah a message for the people of Edom. The Lord said:

*"Look, you have been full of pride in yourselves, but I will make you like nothing among the nations. You will be hated. You think you are safe because your home is in the mountains. You have said, 'Who can bring me down to the ground?' But even though you seem to soar like an eagle and make your nest among the stars, I will bring you down."*

Then God warned,

*"If thieves came to steal from you, they would only take what they wanted. If grape pickers came to take your grapes, they would still leave some grapes behind. But Edom will be plundered, and all your hidden treasures will be taken!*

*"Everyone who has a treaty with you will turn on you. Everyone who is at peace with you will lie to you and attack you. Edom will be destroyed. This is what the Lord says."*

**Christ Connection:** Obadiah had a question for God: "How can you allow Edom to do evil things?" Even though Obadiah didn't understand God's ways, God was still in control. God promised to ultimately rescue His people from their enemies. God showed His people that He is ruler of all the earth, and in the end, Jesus will set up his kingdom and make all things right.

**Big Picture Question:** What is pride?

**Big Picture Answer:** Pride is thinking you are better than others, and it steals glory from God.

The Lord's temple had been destroyed and His people taken away to Babylon. There they stayed in captivity for many years. But God had promised through the prophet Jeremiah that His people would one day return to their own land.

In the first year of Cyrus (SI ruhs), king of Persia, the Lord kept His promise. God put it into the mind of King Cyrus to give this order: "The Lord God of heaven has given me all the kingdoms of the earth and has told me to build Him a house at Jerusalem in Judah. His people may go back to Jerusalem to build His house."

Then King Cyrus brought out all the things that King Nebuchadnezzar had taken from the Lord's house years ago. There were 30 gold basins, 1,000 silver basins, 29 silver knives, 30 gold bowls, 410 silver bowls, and 1,000 other articles. These things were given to God's people.

Thousands and thousands of the Lord's people then left Babylon and traveled back to Jerusalem. They took with them their horses, mules, camels, and donkeys. They were led by a man named Zerubbabel (zee RUB uh BUHL) and a priest named Jeshua (JESH yoo uh).

When they got to Jerusalem, the people brought offerings of gold and silver to help rebuild the house of God. Then, after they had settled themselves in houses and towns, they gathered in Jerusalem. Zerubbabel and Jeshua built an altar to God and began to offer sacrifices on it, as it was written in the law of Moses.

Zerubbabel and Jeshua led the people in clearing the land for the temple. Then they began to build the foundation. When the foundation was finished, the people gathered to celebrate. With trumpets and cymbals, the priests sang praises to God: "For He is good; His faithful love to Israel endures forever." Then all the people gave a great shout of praise to the Lord because the foundation of the Lord's house had been laid.

Many of the older people, who still remembered the first temple, wept loudly, but others shouted with joy. The weeping and shouting was so loud that the noise was heard far away.

**Christ Connection:** Zerubbabel led God's people back to the temple to rebuild it. The temple was the place where God was present. Since Adam and Eve sinned, everything has been affected by sin. The world is not how God wants it to be. One day Jesus will return to lead all of God's people to a greater home—an eternity with Him.

**Big Picture Question:** How did God keep His promise to the Israelites?

**Big Picture Answer:** God changed the heart of the King Cyrus so that the Israelites could go home.

# Haggai, Prophet to Judah

Years before, Zerubbabel (zee RUB uh BUHL) had led God's people back to Jerusalem to rebuild the temple. They had started the work, but had soon stopped because the neighboring peoples did not want God's temple rebuilt. So instead, the people built nice homes for themselves, while God's temple was still in ruins. God was angry with His people because they did not put Him first.

So, in the time of King Darius who ruled over Babylon, the word of the Lord came to Haggai (HA gee i) the prophet. God sent a message through Haggai to Zerubbabel. This is what the Lord said: "These people say: The time has not come for the house of the Lord to be rebuilt. Is it time for you to live in your nice houses, while the Lord's house is in ruins?"

Then God said, "You have planted much but harvested little. You eat but never have enough to be satisfied. You put on clothes but never have enough to get warm. Why? Because My house still lies in ruins, while each of you is busy with his own house." God was telling His people that He had not blessed their work, because they had not put Him first.

Then God said, "Go up into the hills, bring down lumber, and build My house. Then I will be pleased and glorified."

Zerubbabel and all the people obeyed the voice of the Lord and the words of the prophet Haggai. They began to work on the house of God.

Some time later, God again spoke to Haggai the prophet: "Say to Zerubbabel and to all the people: Who remembers the glory of the first temple? How does it look to you now? Doesn't it seem like nothing to you? Even so, be strong, Zerubbabel," said the Lord. "Be strong, all you people of the land. Work! For I am with you. This is the promise I made to you when you came out of Egypt. Don't be afraid."

If the people would only trust in God and put Him first, He would bless them and their work.

**Christ Connection:** God's people had been in a foreign land for a long time with no place to worship God. When the people returned home, Haggai told them to put God first and to rebuild the temple. God promised to be with them. When Jesus came to be with His people, God fulfilled His promise to be with us.

**Big Picture Question:** How can we honor God?

**Big Picture Answer:** We can honor God by putting Him first in our lives.

153

In the time of King Darius, God spoke to the prophet Zechariah (zek uh RI ah) about His people. He said: "The Lord was very angry with your ancestors. But if you will return to Me, then I will return to you."

For in the past, God's people had worshipped false gods. They had lied and cheated and stolen. To punish them, God had let their enemies capture them and take them to other lands. But God was going to bring His people back to their promised land. He would bless them and destroy their enemies. Then God showed Zechariah 8 visions of what would happen.

In the first vision, Zechariah saw a man riding on a red horse. Behind him were other horses. They had been patrolling the earth. Everything was calm—even with His people's enemies. But soon the Lord's house would be rebuilt and His cities would be blessed again.

In the second vision, Zechariah saw 4 horns—these stood for Israel's enemies. Zechariah also saw four craftsmen, who would defeat those enemies. Next, Zechariah saw a man going out to measure Jerusalem—but it could not be measured because it was too large for walls. Instead, the Lord would be a wall of fire around it.

God then showed Zechariah how He would forgive His people if they would follow Him. In the fifth vision, Zechariah saw a solid gold lampstand, which showed how all the Lord's plans would happen because of His power.

Then, Zechariah saw a flying scroll, which was a curse on everyone who disobeyed God. In the seventh vision, a woman sat inside a basket. She represented the wickedness of those who worshipped false gods. She was lifted up and taken back to Babylon. In the eighth vision, Zechariah saw four chariots. Like the horses of the first vision, they would patrol the earth.

God then told Zechariah to collect silver and gold from the people. "Use the gold and silver to make crowns," He said, "and place them on the head of Joshua, the high priest."

Then God spoke to Zechariah about the coming of another king—Jesus. He said: "Look, your King is coming to you. He is humble and riding on the foal of a donkey. He will bring peace to the nations. His kingdom will go to the ends of the earth."

**Christ Connection:** Zechariah used many visions to show the people of God how God was going to restore them. He showed how God would take away the sin of the people and make them whole again through the coming King. Jesus was struck and pierced for people to take away their sin.

**Big Picture Question:** What did Zechariah say about Jesus?

**Big Picture Answer:** Zechariah said Jesus is coming, riding on the foal of a donkey.

Now the building of God's temple in Jerusalem had stopped until the second year of King Darius's rule. Then the prophets Haggai (HA gee i) and Zechariah (zek uh RI ah) spoke to the people, and Zerubbabel (zee RUB uh BUHL) and Jeshua (JESH yoo uh) began again to rebuild God's house.

At that time, the governor of the region came to the Jews and asked, "Who gave you the order to rebuild this temple? And what are the names of the workers who are building it?" Now, the governor didn't stop the building of the temple, but he did send a letter to King Darius to see if the Jews had permission to build it.

In his letter, the governor told King Darius that the Jews had said that Cyrus (who had been king before Darius) had sent them back to the land to rebuild God's house. The governor wrote: If it pleases the king, let a search be made of the royal library in Babylon. Let us see if it is true that King Cyrus ordered the Jews to rebuild the house of God in Jerusalem.

So King Darius ordered that a search be made. The scroll with King Cyrus's order on it was found. So Darius wrote back to the governor: "Leave the building of the house of God alone."

But more than that, King Darius said that the cost of building the temple would be paid for by the taxes from his kingdom. And he ordered the governor to give the Jews whatever they needed—young bulls, rams, lambs, wheat, salt, wine, or oil—to offer sacrifices to God and to pray for the life of the king and his sons.

The governor did just as King Darius ordered, and the Jews continued building God's house. When it was finished, all the Israelites gathered to celebrate. They offered 100 bulls, 200 rams, and 400 lambs, as well as 12 male goats as a sin offering for all Israel— one for each Israelite tribe. They also appointed the priests and the Levites to serve God, as they were told to do in the book of Moses. The Israelites held the Passover feast, and they joyfully celebrated the Festival of Unleavened Bread for seven days. They were joyful because the Lord had caused King Darius to help them in their work and the temple of the Lord was complete!

**Christ Connection:** God's people built the temple so they would have a place to worship God. Years later, God came to earth through His Son, Jesus, to be with His people. Now God dwells not in the temple, but directly with His people. Because of Jesus, we don't need a temple anymore.

**Big Picture Question:** Why did the people build the temple?

**Big Picture Answer:** The people built the temple to worship God.

# Esther Saved Her People

Esther was the queen of King Ahasuerus (ah haz uh EE ruhs), but no one knew she was a Jew. Her uncle was Mordecai (MOR duh ki), who had once saved the king's life. Now, Haman (HAY muhn), a servant of the king, hated Mordecai because he would not bow to him. So Haman plotted to kill not only Mordecai, but all the Jews.

When Mordecai learned of Haman's plan, he tore his clothes and wept. Esther sent a servant to him to see what was wrong. Mordecai told the servant of Haman's plan and begged Esther to go to the king. But Esther said, "If I go to the king without being called, I could be killed. Only if the king holds out his gold scepter to me will I live."

Mordecai answered: "Don't think you'll escape just because you're in the palace. Who knows? Perhaps you were made queen for such a time as this."

So Esther said, "Gather all the Jews and fast for 3 days. My servants and I will do the same. Then, I'll go to the king. If I die, I die."

On the third day, Esther went to the king. He saw her and held out his scepter to her. "Whatever you want, Queen Esther," said the king, "will be given to you—up to half the kingdom."

"Will the king and Haman come to a banquet I've prepared?" Esther said. The king accepted.

At the banquet, he again said, "Whatever you ask for will be given to you." But Esther only asked that they come to another banquet the next day.

Haman left the banquet full of joy, but then he saw Mordecai and was filled with rage again. At home, he told his wife and friends about Mordecai. They said, "Build a gallows, and ask the king to hang Mordecai on it." This pleased Haman, so he had the gallows built.

At the banquet, the king said to Esther again, "Whatever you ask will be given to you."

This time Esther answered, "Please don't let my people and me be killed."

"Who would do such a thing?" demanded the king.

"Haman!" Esther answered.

Then one of the king's servants said, "There is a gallows at Haman's house that he made for Mordecai."

So the king ordered that Haman be hanged on the gallows he had built for Mordecai. Esther and all her people were saved.

**Christ Connection:** Esther spoke to the king for her people in the same way that Jesus speaks to God for us. Haman tried to kill Mordecai, but God was in control and Haman died instead. Likewise, Satan thought he had won when Jesus died on the cross, but God raised Jesus from the dead and defeated Satan once and for all.

**Big Picture Question:** How does God use people?

**Big Picture Answer:** God uses ordinary people to carry out His plans.

Nehemiah (nee uh MI uh) was a Jew living in the court of King Artaxerxes (ahr tuh ZUHRK seez) of Persia. He was the king's cupbearer. One day, Nehemiah's brothers returned from Jerusalem and said to him, "The people there are in great trouble. Jerusalem's wall has been broken down, and its gates have been burned."

When Nehemiah heard this, he sat down and wept. For days, he fasted and prayed to God:

"Yahweh, the God of heaven, let Your eyes be open and Your ears hear my prayer. We have sinned against you. But please remember Your words to Moses: 'If you are unfaithful, I will scatter you among the peoples. But if you return to Me and obey Me, I will gather you from the ends of the earth and bring you to the place I have chosen.' Please, Lord, hear my prayer."

When Nehemiah went to serve the king, he was still sad. He had never been sad in the king's presence before, so the king asked, "Why are you sad, when you aren't sick?"

Nehemiah was overwhelmed with fear and said to the king, "May the king live forever! Why should I not be sad when Jerusalem lies in ruins and its gates have been destroyed by fire?"

Then the king asked, "What do you want?"

Nehemiah prayed to God before he answered the king, "If it pleases the king, send me to Jerusalem so that I may rebuild it."

So the king sent Nehemiah to Jerusalem. He sent with him letters to all the governors so that Nehemiah would have safe travels. He also sent letters to the keeper of the king's forest to give Nehemiah wood to rebuild the gates and the wall of Jerusalem. The king even sent officers from his army to protect Nehemiah.

When Nehemiah had been in Jerusalem three days, he got up one night and inspected the walls of Jerusalem. When he returned, he said to the people there, "You see the trouble we are in. Jerusalem lies in ruins and its gates have been burned down. Come, let's rebuild Jerusalem's wall, so that we will no longer be a disgrace." Then Nehemiah told them how God had helped him, and all that the king had said and done.

So the people said, "Let's start building," and they did.

**Christ Connection:** Nehemiah knew that God would keep His promise to bring His people back home, so he wasn't afraid to help God do it. As Christians, we have a home to look forward to in heaven with God. Jesus is the brave One who goes to His Father for us, and makes the way for us to get home.

**Big Picture Question:** Why was Nehemiah sad?

**Big Picture Answer:** Nehemiah was sad because Jerusalem and its wall were in ruins.

Nehemiah (nee uh MI uh) led the people in rebuilding the wall around Jerusalem. The work was shared among all the different families and tribes.

The high priest and his fellow priests began rebuilding the Sheep Gate. The men of Jericho worked on the section next to them. Other groups worked on the Fish Gate, the Old Gate, the Horse Gate, and all the other gates. Still other workers repaired the towers along the wall.

The workers put in doors, bolts, and bars. Stones were cut and lifted into place. Holes and gaps were filled in. All around the city, people worked. Priest and perfumers, guards and goldsmiths all worked side by side. Soon the wall was already half as tall as it had once been!

When Jerusalem's neighbors—Sanballat (san BAL at), Tobiah, and the Arabs, Ammonites, and Ashdodites (ASH dod ayts)—heard that the repairs were going well, they became furious. They all plotted together to come and fight against Jerusalem.

Nehemiah prayed to God, and then he put guards around the wall day and night.

Jerusalem's enemies said to each other, "They won't know anything is happening until we're already among them. Then we can kill them and stop the work."

But Nehemiah heard about this plan and put people behind the lowest parts of the wall, where it was the weakest. He grouped them by families with their swords, spears, and bows. Then he said to them, "Don't be afraid of your enemies. Remember the greatness of the Lord, and fight for your countrymen, your sons and daughters, your wives and homes."

So the people returned to work on the wall. From that day on, half the men worked while the other half held spears, shields, bows, and armor. The laborers carrying loads worked with one hand and held a weapon with the other. The builders strapped their swords to their sides while they built. Each man carried his own weapon wherever he went.

In this way, the wall was finished in 52 days! When all Jerusalem's enemies heard this, they were afraid, because they knew this had been the work of God.

**Christ Connection:** Nehemiah led the people to rebuild the walls around Jerusalem for protection from their enemies. Jesus came to do more than build a physical wall. He made the way for people to have protection from sin and death by His sacrifice.

**Big Picture Question:** How were God's people protected while they built the wall?

**Big Picture Answer:** Half the people worked while the other half stood ready to fight.

The wall of Jerusalem was finished at last. All the people gathered together in front of the Water Gate—men and women and all the children who were old enough to listen. Then Ezra the priest brought out the book of the law of Moses, and he began to read.

Ezra read from the book of the law from daybreak until noon. All the people listened carefully. Then Ezra praised the Lord, the great God. All the people lifted up their hands and said, "Amen, Amen!" Then they bowed down and worshipped the Lord with their faces to the ground.

The Levites explained the law to the people and helped them understand what was read. Then Nehemiah (nee uh MI uh) the governor, Ezra the priest, and the Levites who were teaching the people said to them, "This day is holy to the Lord your God. Do not mourn or weep." For all the people were weeping as they heard the words of the law.

Then Ezra said to them, "Go and eat what is rich, drink what is sweet, and send food to those who have nothing prepared, because today is holy to our Lord. Do not mourn or be sad, because the joy of the Lord is your stronghold." Then all the people began to eat and drink. There was a great celebration, because they understood the words of God's law that were explained to them.

**Christ Connection:** God's Word is powerful, and it causes people to take action. When Ezra read God's Word, the people changed their ways and grew closer to God. The Bible says that Jesus is "the Word." Jesus is God who came to live with people on earth. Jesus has the power to change our hearts.

**Big Picture Question:** Why did Ezra read God's Word?

**Big Picture Answer:** The laws found in God's Word would help the people obey Him so that they could be holy.

The Jewish people had returned to their promised land, and the temple was rebuilt. But over the years they had become lazy in their worship of God. Now, the Lord loved His people. He wanted them to be holy and to obey Him in all things. So God sent a message to them through His prophet Malachi. God told the people of their sins and called for them to turn back to Him.

The priests were supposed to lead the people in how to worship, but instead they were offering stolen, lame, and sick animals as sacrifices. So the Lord said to them: "I am not pleased with you, and I will accept no offering from your hands."

God also said to priests, "You are supposed to help people follow Me. But you have turned the people away from Me. You have caused many to stumble with your wrong teachings."

God warned the people of a coming day of judgment. He said, "I am going to send My messenger, and he will clear the way before Me. He will be like a fire burning away the sin and waste. He will cleanse the priests, and then they will present pleasing offerings to the Lord."

God then spoke of how the people were robbing Him by not offering to Him a share of their wealth. They had forgotten that everything they had was a gift from God. So God challenged the people, "Bring a tenth of your wealth from the storehouses and give it to Me so that there will be food in My house. Test Me in this! If you obey me, you will see how I open the floodgates of heaven to pour out blessings on you. The blessings will be so great that they cannot be measured."

At that time those who feared the Lord spoke to one another. The Lord noticed them and their names were written in a book of remembrance. "They will be Mine," said the Lord. "And I will have compassion on them. Then you will see the difference between the righteous and the wicked, between one who serves God and one who does not serve Him.

"For the day is coming," said the Lord, "when the wicked will be burned in the fire. But those who fear my Name will rise up on that day which is coming."

**Christ Connection:** The name Malachi means "my messenger." The prophet Malachi came with a message; he told God's people to repent. Malachi also told about another messenger God would send. This messenger, John the Baptist, would call people to repent and prepare them for a third messenger, Jesus Christ, who would bring good news of salvation.

**Big Picture Question:** What did God want the people to do?

**Big Picture Answer:** He wanted them to obey Him and turn back to Him.

# Bible Stories of The New Testament

Jesus is the Son of God, which means that He is fully God. But when Jesus was born on earth, He had human parents too. They were named Mary and Joseph. That means that Jesus was also fully man. So, Jesus was both fully God and fully human—that makes Him different from any other man.

Like all people on the earth, Jesus' family had a history—a family tree. It began all the way back in the Garden of Eden with Adam and Eve. They had a son named Seth, and his son was named Enos. Enos was the great-great-grandfather of Enoch. Enoch walked with God and was also part of Jesus' family. Noah was another member of Jesus' family, along with Abraham, Isaac, and Jacob.

Years later, a man named Salmon was born into Jesus' family tree. He married Rahab, who had saved the spies at the fall of Jericho. They had a son and named him Boaz. He, in turn, married Ruth, who had been so good to her mother-in-law, Naomi. Boaz and Ruth had a son named Obed. Obed's son was named Jesse. Jesse was the father of King David, who was king of all Israel and who was loyal to God. King David wrote many psalms, and some of them spoke of the time when Jesus would come to earth.

Other people in Jesus' family tree were King Solomon and King Jehoshaphat. Then, there were more fathers and more sons. One of them was named Matthan. Matthan had a son named Jacob. Jacob then had a son, and he named him Joseph. And it was this Joseph who became the husband of Mary. Mary gave birth to Jesus, who is called the Messiah.

**Christ Connection:** Jesus is the Son of God, but He also had parents here on earth— Mary and Joseph. Many of the heroes of the Bible were part of Jesus' family—Adam and Eve, Noah, Abraham, Isaac, and Jacob. Rahab and Ruth were also part of Jesus' family, as were King David and his descendants—all the way down to Joseph.

**Big Picture Question:** How is Jesus different from any other man?

**Big Picture Answer:** Jesus is fully God and fully man.

In the days when Herod was King of Judea, there was a priest named Zechariah (zek uh RI ah). His wife's name was Elizabeth. Both Elizabeth and Zechariah loved the Lord and obeyed His laws. But they had no children, and they were both well along in years.

When it was Zechariah's turn to serve as priest before God, he traveled to the temple in Jerusalem. There, he was chosen by lot to enter the sanctuary of the Lord to burn incense. As he went inside, the people gathered outside to pray. Then an angel of the Lord appeared to Zechariah. When Zechariah saw him, he was startled and afraid. But the angel said to him:

*"Don't be afraid, Zechariah, because your prayer has been heard. Your wife Elizabeth will have a son, and you will name him John. There will be joy and delight for you, and many will rejoice at his birth. He will be great in the sight of the Lord and will never drink wine or beer. He will be filled with the Holy Spirit while he is still in his mother's womb. He will turn many of the sons of Israel back to the Lord their God. And he will go before Him in the spirit and power of Elijah, to make the people ready for the Lord's coming."*

"How can I know that this will really happen?" Zechariah asked the angel. "I am an old man, and my wife is not young."

The angel answered, "I am Gabriel, who stands in the presence of God. I was sent to tell you this good news. Now listen! Because you didn't believe my words, you will not be able to speak until the day these things happen."

Meanwhile, the people were waiting outside the temple for Zechariah. They were amazed that he had stayed inside so long. When Zechariah did come out, though, he couldn't speak! That's when the people realized he had seen a vision. He made signs to them, but he still couldn't speak. Zechariah finished the days of his service at the temple and then went back home.

Soon after this, Elizabeth found that she was going to have a baby. "The Lord has done this for me!" she said. "He has looked with favor on me. He has taken away my shame among the people.

**Christ Connection:** Like all the prophets before him, John was used by God for a special purpose. God sent John to be the last of the Old Testament-type prophets who would tell people about the coming Savior. John's job was to remind the people of what God had said in the past and to prepare the hearts of the people to meet Jesus in the future.

**Big Picture Question:** What was John going to do?

**Big Picture Answer:** John was going to tell the people that Jesus was coming.

Long before Jesus was born, the prophets of the Old Testament told of His coming. The prophet Isaiah said this about the birth of Jesus:

*The Lord will give you a sign and this is it: The virgin will have a son, and he will be named Immanuel (which means "God is with us").*

Another time, Isaiah spoke about the kingdom that Jesus would rule over:

*A child will be born for us, and the government will be on His shoulders. He will be named Wonderful Counselor, Mighty God, Eternal Father, Prince of Peace. He will reign on the throne of David and his kingdom will be from now on and forever.*

Isaiah also spoke of how Jesus would be born from the family of Jesse, who was the father of King David:

*Then a shoot will grow from the stump of Jesse, and a branch from his roots will bear fruit. The Spirit of the LORD will rest on Him—a Spirit of wisdom and understanding, a Spirit of counsel and strength, a Spirit of knowledge and of the fear of the LORD.*

The prophet Micah told of how Jesus would be born in Bethlehem:

*Bethlehem, you are small among the tribes of Judah; but One will come from you to be ruler over Israel for Me.*

One by one, each of these prophecies—and many more found in the Old Testament—came true in Jesus.

**Christ Connection:** God's plan to save His people from sin and death was not a secret plan. Though the disobedience of God's people seemed too big of a problem, God had an even bigger solution. God used the prophets to give hope to His people by telling them He was sending a Messiah—born into the world as a baby to live the perfect life Israel failed to live and die the death they—and we—deserve to die.

**Big Picture Question:** What did the prophets tell the people about?

**Big Picture Answer:** The prophets told the people that God would send Jesus, the Messiah to save them from their sins.

## The Angel Speaks to Mary

One day God sent the angel Gabriel to a town in Galilee called Nazareth. The angel went to see a virgin named Mary. She was engaged to a man named Joseph, who was from the family of King David.

Gabriel said to Mary, "Rejoice! You have found favor with God. He is with you."

Mary was troubled, though. What kind of greeting this could be? she wondered. But Gabriel said, "Don't be afraid, Mary. You will have a son, and you will name Him Jesus. He will be great, and He will be called the Son of the Most High. God will give Him the throne of David, and His kingdom will never end."

"How can this be?" Mary asked the angel. "I am not married yet."

Gabriel answered, "The Holy Spirit will come upon you, and God will be the child's father. The baby to be born will be called the Son of God. Remember your relative Elizabeth? She was childless, but now she is going to have a son in her old age. For nothing is impossible with God."

"I belong to God," said Mary. "Let everything happen as you said." Then the angel left her.

Mary hurried to her cousin Elizabeth's house, and she stayed there for three months. Then she went back home.

## The Angel Speaks to Joseph

Now Joseph found out that Mary was pregnant, so he decided to divorce her quietly. He was a kind man, and he did not want to shame Mary in front of everyone.

But an angel of the Lord came to Joseph in a dream. "Joseph, son of David, don't be afraid to take Mary as your wife," the angel said. "The child she is carrying is from the Holy Spirit. She will give birth to a son, and you are to name Him Jesus. He will save His people from their sins."

All of this happened just as the prophet Isaiah had said it would so long ago: "See, the virgin will give birth to a son, and they will name Him "Immanuel," which means "God is with us."

When Joseph woke up from sleeping, he did just as the Lord's angel had told him. He married Mary.

**Christ Connection:** "Therefore, the Lord Himself will give you a sign: The virgin will conceive, have a son, and name him Immanuel" (Isaiah 7:14). The baby Jesus fulfilled Isaiah's prophecy, as well as other prophecies of the coming Savior throughout the Old Testament. Through His life, death, and resurrection, Jesus fulfilled God's plan of redemption that God planned from the beginning of the world.

**Big Picture Question:** What part did Mary and Joseph have in God's plan?

**Big Picture Answer:** God chose Mary and Joseph to be Jesus' parents on earth.

# Mary Visited Elizabeth

After the angel Gabriel visited Mary, she went to see her cousin Elizabeth in the hill country of Judah. Gabriel had told Mary that Elizabeth was going to have a child, even though she was old.

As Mary went in to her cousin's house, she called out to her. And when Elizabeth heard Mary's voice, the baby inside her leaped with joy!

Elizabeth was then filled with the Holy Spirit, and she said to Mary: "You are the most blessed of women, and your child will be blessed!"

"How could such a wonderful thing happen to me?" Elizabeth asked. "How is it that the mother of my Lord should come to me? You see, when I heard your greeting, the baby leaped for joy inside me!"

Then Mary sang this song of praise to God:

*The Lord is great and my spirit rejoices in Him.*

*He has looked on me—His humble servant—with favor.*

*Surely, from now on, all people will call me blessed, because God has done great things for me.*

*His name is holy.*

*He shows mercy to all who have faith in Him.*

*With His mighty arm, He has scattered the proud.*

*He has toppled the mighty from their thrones and lifted up the lowly.*

*He has filled the hungry with good things and sent the rich away empty.*

*He has helped His servant Israel, and He has remembered His promise to Abraham and his descendants.*

Mary stayed with Elizabeth for about 3 months. Then she returned to her home in Nazareth.

**Christ Connection:** Mary's visit to Elizabeth shows us that God was working all things together to bring about the birth of His Son Jesus to be the Savior of the world. Baby John in Elizabeth's womb leaped at the presence of his Savior in the womb of Mary. The mere presence of Jesus, even before He was born, led to rejoicing and praise by everyone there. Through praise and song they worshipped God because of Jesus.

**Big Picture Question:** What did the baby inside Elizabeth do?

**Big Picture Answer:** Elizabeth's baby leaped for joy at the sound of Mary's voice and because of the baby Jesus inside her.

When the time came for Elizabeth to have her baby, she gave birth to a son. All her neighbors and relatives heard of the Lord's goodness to her, and they were happy for her. Eight days after the baby was born, they came to circumcise him. They were going to name him Zechariah (zek uh RI ah), after his father. But Elizabeth said, "No! He will be called John."

"But none of your relatives are called John," they said to her. So they motioned to his father, Zechariah, to find out what he wanted his son to be called. Now, Zechariah had not been able to speak since he had seen the angel in the temple. Zechariah asked for a writing tablet and wrote:

*HIS NAME IS JOHN.*

As soon as Zechariah had written this, his mouth was opened and he could speak again! He began praising God, and the people were all amazed. All throughout the hill country of Judea, everyone talked about these things that had happened. And everyone who heard about John said, "What will this child become?" For the Lord's hand was surely with him.

Then his father Zechariah was filled with the Holy Spirit and he began to prophecy: "Praise the Lord, the God of Israel, because He has given His people a way to be saved. He has raised up the way of salvation for us from the house of His servant, King David, just as He promised long ago.

"He has remembered His holy covenant—the promise that He made to our father Abraham. He has given us the joy of serving Him without fear. This child will be called a prophet of God, because he will go before the Lord to prepare the people for His coming. He will teach the people about salvation through the forgiveness of their sins."

John grew up and was strong in spirit and in faith. He lived in the wilderness until the day he went out to begin preaching to Israel.

**Christ Connection:** A long time before Jesus was born, prophets told God's people that Jesus would come. The prophets also said another man would come first to say, "Jesus is almost here!" The people needed someone to get them ready for Jesus. John the Baptist told people to turn away from their sins because Jesus was coming to be King over the whole world.

**Big Picture Question:** Why was John the Baptist special?

**Big Picture Answer:** John told the people to get ready for the coming of Jesus.

181

# Jesus Was Born

Luke 2:1-20

During the time Mary was pregnant with the baby Jesus, the Roman emperor, Caesar Augustus, ordered everyone to be registered for a census. So every person traveled to the town where his family was from to be counted. Since Joseph was from the family of King David, he and Mary left Nazareth and traveled to Bethlehem, the city of David.

While they were in Bethlehem, the time came for Mary to have her baby. Mary and Joseph looked for a safe place for Mary to have her baby, but every room and inn was full because of all the people who were in town to be counted.

So Mary and Joseph found a place where the animals were kept, and that is where Mary had her baby, Jesus. She wrapped him snugly in cloth, and she laid him in a feeding trough, where the animals ate their food.

Nearby, some shepherds were staying out in the fields to watch over their flocks. It was night and they were protecting the sheep from thieves and wild animals. Suddenly, an angel of the Lord stood before them. A bright light shone all around the shepherds, and they were terrified!

But the angel said to them, "Don't be afraid! I bring you good news of great joy. Today a Savior, who is Messiah the Lord, was born for you in the city of David." Then the angel said, "You will find a baby wrapped snugly in cloth and lying in a feeding trough."

Then the sky was filled heavenly angels singing to God and saying, "Glory to God in the highest heaven, and peace on earth to the people He favors!"

After the angels had left and returned to heaven, the shepherds said to one another, "Let's go straight to Bethlehem and see what has happened. Let's go and see what the Lord has told us about."

The shepherds hurried off to Bethlehem. There they found Mary and Joseph, and the baby who was lying in a feeding trough. After seeing them, the shepherds told Mary and Joseph what the angels had said about this child. Everyone who heard it was amazed at what the shepherds told them.

The shepherds returned to their fields, praising God for all they had seen and heard. Everything had happened just as the angel had said.

**Christ Connection:** The birth of Jesus was good news! Jesus was not an ordinary baby. He was God's Son, sent to earth from heaven. Jesus came into the world to save people from their sins and to be their King.

**Big Picture Question:** Why was Jesus born?

**Big Picture Answer:** Jesus came to save people from their sins.

# Jesus Was Dedicated

On the eighth day after Jesus was born, it was time to present Him to the Lord at the temple, as the law of Moses said. Mary and Joseph brought the baby Jesus up to Jerusalem. At the temple, they offered a sacrifice to the Lord as the law said: a pair of turtledoves or two young pigeons.

Now, there was a man at the temple whose name was Simeon (SIM ee uhn). He was righteous and faithful, and the Holy Spirit was with him. The Holy Spirit had told Simeon that he would not die before he saw the Lord's Messiah, the Savior. When Mary and Joseph brought the baby Jesus into the temple, Simeon saw them. He took Jesus into his arms, praised God, and said:

*"Now, Lord, you can let me die in peace. For my eyes have seen the Savior, just as You promised. You have sent Him to be a light for the Gentiles and a glory to Your people Israel."*

Mary and Joseph were amazed at the things Simeon said about Jesus. Then Simeon blessed them and told His mother Mary: "This child will cause the fall and rise of many in Israel—and a sword will pierce your own soul."

At the temple, there was also a prophetess named Anna. She was a daughter of Phanuel (FAN yoo el), of the tribe of Asher. She was well along in years—for she had lived with her husband 7 years in marriage and had then been a widow for 84 years. Anna never left the temple. She served God night and day with fasting and prayers. At that very moment, she came up and began to thank God and to speak about Jesus to all who would listen.

When Mary and Joseph had done everything according to the law of the Lord, they returned with Jesus to their own town of Nazareth. Jesus grew up and became strong. He was filled with wisdom, and God's grace was on Him.

**Christ Connection:** Throughout the Old Testament, God promised the arrival of a King who would redeem God's people. The people waited for Him and had faith in God's promise. When Jesus arrived, Simeon and Anna knew He was the promised Messiah. Today, we have faith that Jesus is who He said He is and can save us from our sins. We can trust Jesus for our salvation.

**Big Picture Question:** Why were Simeon and Anna waiting?

**Big Picture Answer:** They were waiting for God to send the Savior He had promised.

# The Wise Men Visited Jesus

After Jesus was born in Bethlehem, wise men from the east arrived in Jerusalem. They asked, "Where is the One who has been born King of the Jews? We saw His star in the east and have followed it here so that we may worship him."

King Herod heard about this and was very angry. A new king? He was the only king! Herod called together all the priests and scribes and asked them where this new King would be born.

"In Bethlehem of Judea," they told him. "That is what was written by the prophet Micah."

Herod then secretly sent for the wise men and asked them the exact time that they had first seen the star. Then he sent them on to Bethlehem, saying, "Go and search for the child. When you find Him, tell me so that I can go and worship Him too." But Herod was lying. He didn't want to worship the new King—he wanted to kill Him!

So the wise men went on their way. They followed the star until it led them right to the house where Jesus was. They went inside the house and saw Jesus with Mary, His mother, and they were overjoyed. They fell to their knees and worshipped Him. They gave Jesus gifts of gold, frankincense, and myrrh.

When it was time for the wise men to go, God warned them in a dream not to tell Herod where Jesus was. So they took a different way home.

After the wise men were gone, an angel appeared to Joseph, Mary's husband, in a dream. The angel said, "Get up! Take the child and His mother, and flee to Egypt. Stay there until I tell you. Herod is about to search for the child to kill Him." So in the middle of the night, Joseph got up and took Mary and Jesus to Egypt where they would be safe.

When King Herod saw that he had been tricked by the wise men, he flew into a rage. He ordered that every boy in Bethlehem who was 2 years old and younger be killed! He didn't know that Jesus had already escaped.

Some time later, after Herod died, an angel spoke to Joseph again in a dream. "Get up! Take the child and His mother and go back to Israel. Those who wanted to kill the Child are dead." So Joseph did as the angel said.

**Christ Connection:** The wise men came to worship Jesus as King. Jesus is the King who will rule forever, as God promised to King David in 2 Samuel 7. Jesus is the true King who is worthy of all our worship.

**Big Picture Question:** Why did the wise men visit Jesus?

**Big Picture Answer:** The wise men came to worship Jesus as King.

Every year Mary and Joseph traveled to Jerusalem for the Passover Festival. When Jesus was 12 years old, he went with them.

When the days of the festival were over, Mary and Joseph began their journey home, along with several of their family and friends. Jesus stayed behind in Jerusalem, but His parents didn't know it! They were traveling in a large group, and they thought He was with them.

Mary and Joseph had gone an entire day's journey before they realized that Jesus was missing. They searched for Him among all their relatives and friends. When they couldn't find Him, they hurried back to Jerusalem to look for Him there.

After 3 days, they found Him in the temple. Jesus was sitting among the teachers, listening to them and asking questions. Everyone who heard Him was amazed at His understanding and His answers. When His parents saw Him, they were also amazed.

Mary said to Him, "Son, why have You treated us like this? Your father and I have been worried. We've been searching everywhere for You."

"Why were you searching for Me?" Jesus asked them. "Didn't you know that I had to be in My Father's house?" But Mary and Joseph didn't understand what He was saying to them.

Jesus went home with Mary and Joseph to Nazareth, and He obeyed them. But Mary never forgot about this time in the temple. She kept all these things in her heart and thought about them. And Jesus grew in wisdom and stature, and in favor with God and with people.

**Christ Connection:** Jesus went to the temple to worship because He knew His purpose on earth. He came to be about God's business—teaching, suffering, dying for our sins, and rising again. As God's Son, Jesus died on a cross and was raised to life to save people from their sins.

**Big Picture Question:** Why did Jesus go to the temple?

**Big Picture Answer:** Jesus went to the temple to be in His Father's house.

# Jesus Was Baptized

John the Baptist was at the Jordan River. He told everyone who would listen that the Lord was coming and the kingdom of heaven was near. John was baptizing people in the river as they confessed their sins. Jesus came from Galilee to see John at the Jordan River, because He wanted to be baptized by him.

John didn't think he should baptize Jesus, though. "I need to be baptized by You!" John told Him. "Why do you want me to baptize you?"

Jesus answered him, "Do this, because this is what the Lord wants." So John baptized Jesus.

As soon as Jesus came up out of the water, He saw the heavens being torn open. The Spirit of God came down to Him like a dove. Then a voice from heaven spoke and said,

*This is My beloved Son.*
*I take great joy in Him!*

**Christ Connection:** Jesus' baptism shows us that Jesus completely obeyed God and identified with sinners by being baptized like sinners are baptized. His baptism was a symbol or sign that He would obey God and take on the punishment for the sins of the world. His baptism points to His death on the cross. He is the only One who can save us.

**Big Picture Question:** Why was Jesus baptized?

**Big Picture Answer:** Jesus was baptized to show the people that He was willing to obey God.

After Jesus was baptized, He was led by the Holy Spirit into the wilderness to be tempted by the Devil. For 40 days and 40 nights, Jesus fasted. He ate nothing during those days. When those days were over, He was hungry.

The Devil came to Jesus. He knew Jesus was very hungry, so he said, "If You are the Son of God, tell this stone to become bread."

But Jesus answered, "It is written: Man must not live on bread alone but on every word that comes from the mouth of God."

The Devil then took Jesus to the holy city of Jerusalem. There, he had Him stand on the highest point of the temple. The Devil said to Him, "If You are the Son of God, throw Yourself down. For it is written: He will give His angels orders about you. They will hold you with their hands so that you will not strike your foot against a stone."

But Jesus told him, "It is also written: Do not test the Lord your God."

Then the Devil took Jesus to a very high mountain and showed Him all the kingdoms of the world and their splendor. And the Devil said to Him, "I will give you all the riches and power of these kingdoms. They have been given to me, and I can give them to anyone I want. It will all be Yours if You will fall down and worship me."

Jesus said, "Go away, Satan! For it is written: Worship the Lord your God, and serve only Him."

After the Devil had finished every temptation, he left Jesus for a time. Then the angels came and began to serve Jesus.

**Christ Connection:** Jesus responded to the Devil's tempting with Scripture and unwavering faith. Although Jesus faced temptation, He never sinned. Jesus was perfect and righteous. A perfect sacrifice was required to cover sin. Jesus was that perfect sacrifice for us when He died on the cross.

**Big Picture Question:** How did Jesus deal with temptation?

**Big Picture Answer:** Jesus used the words of God to beat temptation and the Devil.

# Jesus Called His Disciples

Matthew 4:18–22; 9:9–13; Mark 1:16–20; 2:13–14; 3:13–19; Luke 5:27–32; 6:12–16

John the Baptist was arrested by King Herod. When Jesus heard this news, He went to Galilee and began preaching the good news of God.

"The kingdom of God has come near," He said. "Repent—turn away from your sins—and believe in the good news."

As Jesus was walking along the Sea of Galilee, He saw two brothers. They were Simon, who was called Peter, and his brother Andrew. They were fishermen, and they were casting a net into the sea.

Jesus said to them, "Follow Me, and I will teach you to fish for people!" Peter and Andrew immediately left their nets and followed Him.

Going on from there, Jesus saw two other brothers, James and his brother John. They were in a boat mending their nets, along with their father, Zebedee. Jesus called to them. They, too, immediately left the boat and their father, and they followed Jesus.

As Jesus went on, He saw a man named Matthew (who was also called Levi) sitting at the tax office. Jesus said to him, "Follow Me!" So Matthew left everything behind, and he got up and followed Him.

Then Matthew held a great feast for Jesus at his house. Many tax collectors and sinners were invited to eat with Jesus and His disciples. When the Pharisees saw this, they asked His disciples, "Why does your Teacher eat with tax collectors and sinners?"

Jesus heard what the Pharisees were asking. "Those who are healthy don't need a doctor," He said, "but the sick do. Go and learn what this means: I want mercy, not sacrifice. I haven't come to call the righteous, but rather the sinners to turn back to God."

During those days, Jesus went up to the mountain to pray. He spent all night in prayer to God. When daylight came, He called for His disciples. Then He chose 12 of them to be with Him as His apostles. They were: Simon, to whom He gave the name Peter, and Andrew his brother; James and John, who were called the "Sons of Thunder"; Philip and Bartholomew; Matthew and Thomas; James the son of Alphaeus, and Thaddaeus; Simon the Zealot, and Judas Iscariot, who would betray Jesus.

**Christ Connection:** Jesus taught His disciples to teach others about Him. The good news about Jesus was too great not to share with the entire world! Jesus came to save people from their sin.

**Big Picture Question:** What did Jesus ask His disciples to do?

**Big Picture Answer:** Follow Him and tell others about Him.

There was a Pharisee named Nicodemus. He was a ruler of the Jews. One night, Nicodemus came to Jesus to talk to Him. He wanted to know more about who this Jesus really was.

Nicodemus said, "Rabbi, we know that You have come from God as a teacher. No one could do the miracles You do unless God were with him."

Jesus said, "I tell you: Unless someone is born again, he cannot see the kingdom of God."

Nicodemus didn't understand. "But how can anyone be born again when he is old?" he asked. "Can he go back into his mother's womb and be born a second time?"

Jesus answered, "A man cannot enter the kingdom of God unless he is born of water and the Spirit. Whatever is born of the flesh is flesh, and whatever is born of the Spirit is spirit. Do not be amazed because I told you that you must be born again."

"How can these things be?" asked Nicodemus. He still didn't understand.

"Are you a teacher of Israel and you don't know these things?" Jesus asked. "If I've told you about things that happen on earth and you don't believe Me, then how will you believe Me if I tell you about things of heaven? No one has gone up into heaven except the One who came down from heaven—the Son of Man. Everyone who believes in Him will have eternal life."

Then Jesus said, "God loved the world so much that He sent His One and Only Son to save the world. God didn't send His Son to judge the world guilty. God sent His Son to save the world through Him. Anyone who believes in Him is saved, but anyone who doesn't believe is already found guilty.

"This is the truth: The light has come into the world. But the people loved the darkness instead of the light. This is because the things they did were evil. Everyone who does evil things hates the light and stays away from it, so that his evil deeds can't be seen. But those who live by the truth come to the light, so that everyone can see that what he does is through God."

**Christ Connection:** Without Jesus, we are spiritually dead. Sin separates us from God. When God graciously gives people the Holy Spirit, they are "born again"—they receive new life and become God's children. Jesus offers new life to those who trust in Him for salvation.

**Big Picture Question:** How do you know God loves you?

**Big Picture Answer:** God sent His One and Only Son, Jesus, to save me.

# Jesus and John the Baptist

Jesus and His disciples went to the Judean countryside. There, He spent time with His disciples, teaching and baptizing the people who came to Him. John also was baptizing people in Aenon (EE non), near Salim, because there was plenty of water there. (This was before John was thrown into prison.)

Then John's disciples began to argue with a certain Jew about purification—which is a kind of cleansing for religious reasons. So the disciples came to John and said, "Rabbi, the One you talked about—Jesus—is baptizing people. Everyone is going to Him."

John said, "You know that I said, 'I am not the Messiah, but I've been sent ahead of Him.' It's just like it is at a wedding: The one who has the bride is the groom. The groom's friend stands by and listens for the groom, and he has great joy when he hears the groom's voice. In the same way, my joy is now complete. Jesus—the groom—is here. Jesus must become greater, while I must become less."

The one who is from the earth talks about the things of the earth. But the One who comes from heaven is above all others. He tells of all that He has seen and heard, but no one believes what He says! Those who do believe Him know that God is true. For God sent Him, and He speaks God's words.

The Father loves the Son, and He has given all things to His Son. Those who believe in the Son will have eternal life. But those who do not believe will not see that life. And the anger of God will be on them.

**Christ Connection:** John the Baptist was baptizing when Jesus' disciples came and asked him about Him. John told them he was not the Messiah and had only come to prepare the way for Him. Now that Jesus had come, John's mission was complete.

**Big Picture Question:** Why did John say he must become less?

**Big Picture Answer:** Jesus had come and it was time for Him to teach the people, instead of John.

The Pharisees heard that Jesus was baptizing more disciples than John. (Now, Jesus Himself was not baptizing, but His disciples were.) So Jesus left Judea and went back to Galilee. He had to travel through Samaria, where Jacob's well was. Jesus was worn out from His journey, so He sat down at the well. It was about 6 in the evening.

A woman of Samaria came to get water from the well.

"Give Me a drink," Jesus said to her. (His disciples had gone into town to buy food.)

The woman was surprised. Jews did not speak to Samaritans. "Why do You—a Jew—ask for a drink from a Samaritan woman?" she asked Him.

Jesus answered, "If you knew who was asking you for a drink, you would ask Me for a drink. And I would give you living water."

"You don't even have a bucket," said the woman, "and the well is deep. So where do You get this 'living water'?"

Jesus said, "Everyone who drinks this water from the well will get thirsty again. But whoever drinks from the water that I give him will never be thirsty again—ever! In fact, the water I give him will become a well of eternal life." Now Jesus was speaking about the Holy Spirit, but the woman didn't understand that.

"Sir," the woman said, "give me this water so I won't get thirsty again. Then I won't have to come back here to the well to get water."

"Go get your husband," Jesus told her.

"I don't have a husband," she said.

"That's right. You don't have a husband," Jesus said. "You've had five husbands, and the man you are with now is not your husband."

"I see You are a prophet," the woman said. "Our fathers worshipped on this mountain, but the Jews say that the place to worship is in Jerusalem."

Jesus told her, "You Samaritans don't know what you worship. We do know what we worship, because salvation is from the Jews. But the time has come when true worshippers will worship the Father in spirit and truth. The Father wants people to worship Him that way. God is spirit, so those who worship Him must worship in spirit and truth."

The woman said, "I know that the Messiah (called Christ) is coming. When He comes, He will explain everything to us."

"I am the Messiah," Jesus said.

**Christ Connection:** Jesus offered the woman something no one else could give her—living water. Jesus wasn't talking about water that would satisfy her physical thirst; Jesus was talking about the Holy Spirit who would satisfy her spiritual thirst. Jesus gives the Holy Spirit to those who come to Him by faith.

**Big Picture Question:** What did Jesus offer the woman?

**Big Picture Answer:** Jesus offered her the living water of the Holy Spirit.

# Jesus Returned to Nazareth

Jesus came to Nazareth, the town where He had grown up. As usual, He entered the synagogue on the Sabbath and stood up to read. The scroll of the prophet Isaiah was given to Him. He unrolled the scroll and found the place where it was written:

*"The Spirit of the Lord is on Me. He has anointed Me to preach good news to the poor. He has sent Me to declare the captives will be released and the blind will see. The oppressed will the freed. This is the year of the Lord's favor."*

Jesus then rolled up the scroll. He gave it back to the attendant and sat down. The eyes of everyone in the synagogue were fixed on Him. He then said to them, "Today as you listen, this Scripture has been fulfilled."

They had all been speaking well of Him and were amazed by the words that came from His mouth, but they said, "Isn't this Joseph's son?"

Then He said to them, "No doubt you will quote this proverb to Me: 'Doctor, heal yourself. So all the miracles we've heard about that took place in Capernaum (kuh PUHR nee uhm), do them here in Your hometown too.'"

Jesus also said, "But no prophet is believed in his hometown. I tell you that there were many widows in Israel in days of Elijah when it didn't rain for three years and six months. And though there was a terrible famine all over the land, Elijah was not sent to help anyone in Israel. Instead he was sent to a widow at Zarephath (ZER uh fath). And in the prophet Elisha's time, there were many in Israel who had leprosy. But not one of them was healed. Only Naaman (NAY uh muhn) the Syrian was healed."

When the people in the synagogue heard this, they were very angry. They got up and drove Jesus out of town. They brought Him to the edge of the hill that their town was built on. There, they planned to throw Him over the cliff! But Jesus slipped right through the crowd and went on His way.

**Christ Connection:** Hundreds of years before Jesus was born, the prophet Isaiah wrote about God's plan to send a Messiah who would bring good news and redeem people who were broken and hurting. Jesus read Isaiah's words and told everyone who was listening that He is the promised Messiah.

**Big Picture Question:** Who did Jesus say He was?

**Big Picture Answer:** Jesus said He was the Messiah whom God had promised to send.

# Jesus Healed an Official's Son

Jesus went again to Cana of Galilee. (This is where He had turned water into wine at the wedding feast—which was His first miracle.)

Now there was a certain royal official whose son was sick at Capernaum (kuh PUHR nee uhm). When this man heard that Jesus had come into Galilee, he hurried to see Him. The man begged Jesus to come and heal his son, because he was about to die.

"Unless you people see signs and wonders, you will not believe," Jesus told him.

But the official begged, "Sir, please come down before my boy dies!"

Jesus didn't go with him, but He said, "Go. Your son will live." The man believed what Jesus said to him and hurried back home.

While the man was still on his way home, his slaves came to meet him. "Your son is alive!" they said. The man asked them at what time his son had gotten better. "Yesterday, at seven in the morning, the fever left him," they answered. The father was amazed. That was the very same time that Jesus had told him, "Your son will live." Then the man himself believed and so did his entire household.

This, then, was the second miracle Jesus performed after He came from Judea to Galilee.

**Christ Connection:** The official wanted Jesus to deliver his son from death, and it was not until Jesus did so that he understood who Jesus is—the promised Messiah. It took faith for the official to believe Jesus' words—that his son was healed. In healing the official's son, Jesus showed His authority and power as God's Son.

**Big Picture Question:** What did the official want Jesus to do?

**Big Picture Answer:** The official wanted Jesus to heal his son.

# Jesus Drove Out Unclean Spirits
Mark 1:21-28; Luke 4:31-37

Jesus and His disciples went into Capernaum (kuh PUHR nee uhm). On the Sabbath, He went to the synagogue and began to teach. The people were amazed at His teaching. Unlike the scribes, Jesus taught them as one who had authority.

In the synagogue, there was a man with an unclean spirit. Just then, he cried out in a loud voice, "What do You want to do with us, Jesus of Nazareth? Have You come to destroy us? I know who You are—the Holy One of God!"

But Jesus stopped him and said, "Be quiet, and come out of him!" The unclean spirit shook the man and threw him to the ground. Then it shouted with a loud voice and came out of him without hurting him at all.

The people watching were all amazed! They kept saying to each other, "What is this new message? He teaches with authority. He tells even the unclean spirits to come out, and they obey Him!"

The news about Jesus began to spread all over Galilee.

**Christ Connection:** Jesus is the King who has come to make all things right. By commanding the unclean spirit to come out of the man, Jesus showed He is greater than all our enemies. One day Jesus will take away Satan, sin, and death once and for all.

**Big Picture Question:** Who did the man with unclean spirit say that Jesus was?

**Big Picture Answer:** He said Jesus was the Holy One of God.

# Jesus Healed Peter's Mother-in-Law

As soon as Jesus and His disciples left the synagogue at Capernaum (kuh PUHR nee uhm), they went to Peter and Andrew's house. James and John came with them. Peter's mother-in-law was there, lying in bed with a high fever. They told Jesus about her. So Jesus went in to see her. He touched her hand and raised her up. The fever left her, and she began to serve them.

When evening came, the people brought to Jesus many who were sick and possessed by demons. He drove out the spirits with a word and healed all who were sick. This was so that the words of the prophet Isaiah would be made true: "He Himself took our weaknesses and carried our diseases."

**Christ Connection:** The prophet Isaiah wrote that the promised Messiah would bear our sickness and carry our pain. Jesus fulfilled this prophecy as He healed people. Sickness exists because of sin. One day, when Jesus returns, there will be no more sickness because Jesus dealt with sin on the cross.

**Big Picture Question:** What did the prophet Isaiah say about Jesus?

**Big Picture Answer:** Isaiah said that Jesus would bear our sickness and carry our pain.

# Jesus Cleansed a Leper

Matthew 8:1–4; Mark 1:35–45; Luke 5:12–16

Very early one morning, Jesus went up on the mountain to pray. When He came down from the mountain, large crowds had gathered and began to follow Him. While he was in one of the towns, a man with a serious skin disease—a leper—came up and fell down to his knees in front of Jesus. The man begged Him, "Lord, if You are willing, You can make me clean."

Jesus was moved with compassion and felt sorry for the man. He reached out His hand and touched him, saying, "I am willing. Be clean."

Instantly the disease left him, and He was healed! Then Jesus told him, "Don't tell anyone. But go and show yourself to the priest. Then offer the gift that Moses commanded for your cleansing."

But the man went out and began telling everyone what had happened. So many people came to hear Jesus and to be healed that He could no longer enter a town openly. So Jesus went out to the deserted places, and the people came to Him from all around.

**Christ Connection:** Not only did Jesus have the power to make a leper clean, He was willing to make him clean. Like the disease of leprosy, sin deeply affects all people and makes them spiritually dead. Jesus willingly died on the cross and rose from the dead to save us from our sin and give us new life.

**Big Picture Question:** What did Jesus tell the man with the skin disease after He had healed him?

**Big Picture Answer:** Jesus told the man not to tell anyone and to go and show himself to the priests.

Jesus came back to Capernaum (kuh PUHR nee uhm). When the people heard this, they gathered at the house where He was staying. On one of those days, while He was teaching, many Pharisees and teachers of the law came to hear Him. A great many others came to hear Him too. So many people gathered to hear Jesus that there was no more room in the house. Even the doorway was filled with people.

At that time, 4 men came to see Jesus. They were carrying a man on a mat. The man was paralyzed. The four men were hoping that Jesus would heal their friend. They tried to bring him in and set him down in front of Jesus, but they couldn't even get in the door because of the crowd. So the men went up on the roof. They took off the roof tiles above where Jesus was. When they had broken through the roof, they lowered their friend on his mat. They lowered him down, right into the middle of the crowd and right in front of Jesus!

Seeing the friends' faith, Jesus told the paralyzed man, "Friend, your sins are forgiven."

But some of the scribes and Pharisees sitting there began to think to themselves: "Who is this man? Why does He speak like this? He's blaspheming and saying things against God! Who can forgive sins except God alone?"

Right away Jesus knew that they were thinking, and He said to them, "Why are you thinking these evil things in your hearts? Which is easier to say, 'Your sins are forgiven,' or to say, 'Get up, pick up your mat, and walk'? But just so you will know that the Son of Man has the authority on earth to forgive sins," He turned to the paralyzed man and said, "Get up, pick up your mat, and go home."

Immediately the man got up, picked up his mat, and walked out in front of everyone, praising God. The people were amazed! They praised God, saying, "We have never seen anything like this!"

**Christ Connection:** The man who was paralyzed had a great need—to be healed. Jesus knew this and did something even greater; Jesus forgave his sins and then He healed the man. Because Jesus is God, He has the power and authority to heal and forgive. Jesus offers forgiveness to those who know and love Him.

**Big Picture Question:** What did the paralyzed man need?

**Big Picture Answer:** The paralyzed man needed to be healed *and* forgiven.

On the Sabbath, Jesus went to the synagogue and began teaching. There was a man there whose right hand was paralyzed.

Now the scribes and the Pharisees were watching Jesus closely. They wanted to see if He would heal the man's hand on the Sabbath, so that they could find something to accuse Jesus of. (It was against the Jewish law to do work on the Sabbath.) So the scribes and the Pharisees asked Him, "Is it lawful to heal on the Sabbath?"

But Jesus knew what they were thinking. He said to the man with the paralyzed hand, "Get up and stand here." So the man got up and stood where Jesus told him. Then Jesus said to the scribes and Pharisees, "I ask you: Is it lawful to do what is good on the Sabbath or to do what is evil? Is it lawful to save a life or to destroy it?"

Then Jesus gave them an example: "If a man had a sheep that fell into a pit on the Sabbath day, wouldn't he lift it out? And a man is worth far more than a sheep, so it is lawful to do what is good on the Sabbath."

Jesus looked around at them all. He saw the hardness of their hearts, and it made Him both sad and angry. Then He said to the man, "Stretch out your hand." He did so, and his hand was healed. But instead of being happy for the man, the scribes and Pharisees were filled with rage. They began plotting together about what they might do to destroy Jesus.

**Christ Connection:** Jesus showed that God's laws were meant to help people, not to hurt them. Jesus acted in love, even on the Sabbath. The religious leaders plotted against Jesus to kill Him—an act God planned to show His love to the whole world by providing forgiveness and salvation through Jesus' death on the cross.

**Big Picture Question:** What are God's laws meant to do?

**Big Picture Answer:** God's laws are meant to help people, not to hurt them.

The crowds gathered to hear Jesus. When He saw them, Jesus went up on the mountain. There, He sat down and began to teach. He taught the people about how to live, how to treat each other, and how to love God.

Jesus taught about the blessings of believing in Him:

The poor in spirit are blessed, for the kingdom of heaven is theirs.

Those who mourn are blessed, for they will be comforted.

The gentle are blessed, for they will inherit the earth.

Those who hunger and thirst for righteousness are blessed, for they will be filled.

The merciful are blessed, for they will be shown mercy.

The pure in heart are blessed, for they will see God.

The peacemakers are blessed, for they will be called sons of God.

Those who are persecuted for righteousness are blessed, for the kingdom of heaven is theirs.

Jesus compared His believers to salt and light:

"You are the salt of the earth," He said. "But if the salt should lose its taste, it's no longer good for anything. You are the light of the world. No one lights a lamp and hides it under a basket. Let your light shine before men, so that they will see your good works and give glory to God."

Jesus taught the people about how to follow Him:

"Love your enemies, and pray for them."

"Whenever you give to the poor, give in secret. And when you pray, don't pray just so that people will hear you."

"Forgive others. If you forgive those who sin against you, God will forgive you as well. But if you don't forgive them, God will not forgive you."

"Don't collect treasures on earth, which can be destroyed or stolen. Collect treasures in heaven instead. For where your treasure is, that's where your heart will be also.

"Don't worry about your life or what you will eat or drink or wear. Look at the birds: They don't sow or reap or gather into barns, yet God feeds them. Aren't you worth more than birds? Seek the kingdom of God and His righteousness first, and all these things that you need will be given to you."

Jesus taught the people many, many things. When He finished teaching, the crowds were amazed because He taught them like one who had authority, and not like their scribes.

**Christ Connection:** The scribes and Pharisees looked righteous on the outside, but Jesus taught His disciples about a righteousness that comes from the inside. People who know and love Jesus have changed hearts that want to honor Jesus because they are grateful for His gift of salvation.

**Big Picture Question:** What did Jesus teach the people about their enemies?

**Big Picture Answer:** People should love their enemies and pray for them.

Jesus traveled from one town and village to another, preaching the good news of the kingdom of God. One day, He was sitting by the sea. Such large crowds gathered that He got into a boat and sat down to teach.

Jesus told the people many things in parables. In one of those parables, Jesus compared the sharing of God's words to a sower of seeds.

Jesus said, "A sower went out to sow his seed. As he was sowing, some seed fell along the path, and the birds came and ate it up. Other seed fell on rocky ground, where there wasn't much soil. It sprang up quickly since the soil wasn't deep. But when the sun came up it was scorched. Because it had no root, it withered and died. Other seed fell among thorns, and the thorns grew up and choked it. Still other seed fell on good ground. When it sprang up, it produced a crop: sometimes 100, sometimes 60, and sometimes 30 times more than what was sown."

Then Jesus' disciples asked Him, "What does this parable mean?" So He said, "The secrets of the kingdom of God are for you to know. But to others, everything is in parables. This is so that, 'Looking they may not see, and hearing they may not understand.'

"So listen to this parable of the sower. The sower is the one who sows the word of God. The seed that fell along the path are those people who have heard the word and don't understand it. The Devil comes and snatches the word away from their hearts, so that they will not believe and be saved.

"The seed that fell on rocky ground are those people who hear the word and welcome it with joy. But they have no roots in the word, so when hard times come because of the word, they stumble.

"Now the seed that fell among the thorns—these are the people who hear the word and go on their way. Then they are choked with the worries, riches, and pleasures of life, and they produce no fruit.

"But the seed that falls on the good ground—these are the people who hear and understand the word with an honest and good heart. They hold on to it, and it bears fruit in their lives—sometimes 100, 60, or 30 times what was sown."

**Christ Connection:** When people hear the truth about Jesus, not everyone believes it. Some don't understand it, some believe in Jesus for selfish reasons, and some only want part of Jesus because they love other things more. But those who hear the gospel and understand that Jesus is God who saves sinners will become like Jesus and share His good news with others.

**Big Picture Question:** What was the seed being sown?

**Big Picture Answer:** The seed was the word of God.

Many tax collectors and sinners came to listen to Jesus. The Pharisees and scribes complained, "This Jesus welcomes sinners and eats with them!"

### The Parable of the Lost Sheep

So Jesus said, "If a man has 100 sheep and loses one of them, doesn't he leave the 99 to go after the lost one? And when he finds it, he calls to his friends, saying, 'Rejoice with me! I've found my lost sheep!' In the same way, there's more joy in heaven over one sinner who repents than over 99 righteous people who don't need to repent.

### The Parable of the Lost Coin

"Or if a woman loses one of her 10 silver coins, doesn't she search until she finds it? Then when she finds it, she calls out, saying, 'Rejoice with me! I've found my coin!' In the same way, God's angels rejoice over one sinner who comes back to God."

### The Parable of the Lost Son

Jesus also said: "A man had 2 sons. The younger son said to his father, 'Give me my inheritance now.' So the father did. The younger son traveled to a distant country and wasted his money on foolish living.

"After the son had spent everything, a famine struck that country. He could only find work feeding pigs. He was so hungry, he longed to eat the pigs' food. He said to himself, 'I'm dying of hunger! But My father's servants have more than enough food! I'll go to my father and say, I have sinned against you. I'm not worthy to be your son. Make me like one of your servants.'

"So he got up and went to his father. When the father saw him coming, he ran to him and kissed him. The son said, 'Father, I've sinned against you. I'm not worthy to be called your son.'

"But the father told his slaves, 'Quick! Bring out the best robe for him and kill the fattened calf. We must celebrate!'

"The older son saw this and refused to go to the feast. His father pleaded, but he said, 'I've never disobeyed you, yet you've never given me a celebration with my friends. But this son—who wasted your money—comes back and you kill the fattened calf for him!'

"'Son,' the father said, 'everything I have is yours. But we had to celebrate. Your brother was lost and now he's found.'"

**Christ Connection:** A shepherd was seeking his sheep, a woman was seeking her coin, and a father was seeking his prodigal son. Jesus told these parables to teach about Himself. As Savior, Jesus seeks sinners and paid the ultimate price—His own life—to save us.

**Big Picture Question:** What does Jesus search for?

**Big Picture Answer:** Jesus searches for sinners who are lost, so that He can save them.

One day, as evening came, Jesus and His disciples got into a boat.

Jesus said to them, "Let's cross over to the other side of the sea."

So they set out. As they were sailing, Jesus fell asleep on a cushion in the back of the boat. Suddenly a terrible storm rose up on the sea. The wind roared and the waves crashed over the side of the boat. The disciples were terrified! They had seen many storms before, but they were afraid this one might sink their boat.

The disciples went to Jesus and woke Him up, saying, "Lord, save us! We're going to die!"

But Jesus said to them, "Why are you afraid? Do you still have no faith?"

Then Jesus got up and said to the wind and the waves, "Silence! Be still!" And they stopped! There was a great calm on the sea.

The disciples were amazed. "What kind of man is this?" they asked each other. "Even the winds and the waves obey Him!"

**Christ Connection:** Who is this Jesus? Jesus' disciples knew He was a good man and a good teacher; when Jesus calmed the wind and the waves, He showed His disciples that He is also God. God rules the sea and stills its waves (Psalm 89:9).

**Big Picture Question:** What does Jesus have power over?

**Big Picture Answer:** Jesus has power over the wind and the waves and all of creation.

# Jesus Fed Five Thousand

Matthew 14:13–21; Mark 6:30–44; Luke 9:10–17; John 6:1–14

Jesus and His disciples had been teaching and healing many people. There were so many people coming and going that they didn't even have time to eat! So Jesus said to His disciples, "Come away with Me to a quiet place and rest for a while."

So Jesus and His disciples got into a boat to go away by themselves, but many people saw them leaving. The people followed them on foot and arrived ahead of them. When Jesus stepped out of the boat, He saw the huge crowd. He felt sorry for them, because they were like sheep without a shepherd. So He began to teach them many things.

When evening came, the disciples went to Jesus and said, "This place is a wilderness, and it's already late. Send the crowds away so they can go into the villages and buy food for themselves."

"They don't need to go away," Jesus told them. "You give them something to eat."

Philip said, "Even a year's worth of wages wouldn't buy enough bread for each of them to have even a bite."

Then Jesus asked, "How many loaves do you have? Go and look."

Andrew, who was Peter's brother, said, "There's a boy here who has 5 barley loaves and 2 fish—but what are they for so many?"

"Bring them here to Me," Jesus said, "and have the people sit down."

There was plenty of grass in that place, so the crowds of people sat down. There were about 5,000 men, plus women and children. Jesus took the 5 loaves and the 2 fish. Looking up to heaven, He blessed them. Then He broke the loaves and gave them to the disciples. The disciples gave them to the crowds, along with the fish. Everyone ate as much as they wanted.

When the people were full, Jesus told His disciples, "Pick up the leftover pieces so that nothing is wasted." The disciples filled 12 baskets with pieces of the leftover bread!

When the people saw what Jesus had done, they said, "This really is the Prophet who was to come into the world!"

**Christ Connection:** By feeding the 5,000, Jesus provided for the physical needs of the crowd. The next day, Jesus called Himself the bread of life (John 6:36). Only Jesus is able to satisfy our souls by providing forgiveness, friendship with God, and eternal life.

**Big Picture Question:** Why did Jesus feel sorry for the people?

**Big Picture Answer:** Jesus felt sorry for them because they were like sheep without a shepherd.

# Jesus Healed a Blind Man

Matthew 20:29-34;
Mark 10:46-52; Luke 18:35-43

As Jesus and His disciples were leaving Jericho, there was a blind man named Bartimaeus (bahr tih MEE uhs) sitting by the road begging. Hearing a crowd passing by, he asked what was happening. "Jesus the Nazarene is passing by," they told him.

So the blind man called out, "Jesus, Son of David, have mercy on me!" Many people told him to be quiet, but he kept calling out all the more, "Son of David, have mercy on me!"

Jesus stopped and ordered that the man be brought to Him.

The people called to Bartimaeus and said, "Have courage! Get up—He's calling for you. So Bartimaeus threw off his coat, jumped up, and came to Jesus.

Jesus asked him, "What do you want Me to do for you?"

"Lord," the blind man said, "I want to see!"

"Receive your sight!" Jesus told him. "Your faith has healed you."

Instantly, the man could see! He began to follow Jesus, praising and glorifying God. When the people saw that Bartimaeus had been healed, they also praised God. Jesus had power over sickness!

**Christ Connection:** The prophet Isaiah wrote that the promised Messiah would open blind eyes (Isaiah 35:5; 42:7). He was here! Jesus was the promised Messiah, and He opened the eyes of the blind. This miracle is a picture of another way Jesus opens blind eyes. As sinners, we are blind to the truth about God until Jesus opens our eyes and saves us.

**Big Picture Question:** What does Jesus have power over?

**Big Picture Answer:** Jesus has power over sickness.

# Jesus Drove Out Demons

Jesus and His disciples sailed to the other side of the sea, to the region of the Gerasenes, which is across from Galilee. As soon as Jesus stepped out of the boat, a man who was possessed by demons came out of the tombs to meet Him.

For a long time, the man had not worn any clothes, and he had lived in the tombs instead of a house. The people had often bound him with shackles and chains, but he snapped off the chains and smashed the shackles. No one was strong enough to control him. Night and day, he cried out among the tombs. He roamed the mountains and cut himself with stones.

When the man saw Jesus, he ran and fell down before Him. Then he cried out, "What do You have to do with me, Jesus, Son of the Most High God? I beg You, don't torment me!" For Jesus had said, "Come out of the man, you unclean spirit!"

"What is your name?" Jesus asked him.

"My name is Legion," he said. This was because there were many demons inside him. The demons begged Jesus not to send them to the abyss.

Nearby, there was a large herd of pigs, feeding on the hillside. The demons pleaded with Him, "Send us into the pigs." So Jesus did.

The demons came out of the man and went into the pigs, but then the herd of about 2,000 pigs rushed down the steep bank into the sea and drowned there! When the men who tended the pigs saw what happened, they ran off and reported it in the town and countryside.

People came to see what had happened. They saw Jesus and with him was the man the demons had come out of. He was sitting at Jesus' feet, dressed and in his right mind. The eyewitnesses told them what had happened to the man and to the pigs. Then all the people asked Jesus to leave them, because they afraid. So Jesus got into the boat to leave.

As Jesus was getting into the boat, the man who had been demon-possessed begged to go with Him. But Jesus sent him away and said, "Go back to your home. Tell everyone what God has done for you." So off he went, telling everyone all that Jesus had done for him—and they were all amazed.

**Christ Connection:** We can have hope in a world affected by evil because Jesus has power over evil. While no one had the strength to control the man with the demons, Jesus did. Jesus used His power to free the man. Jesus is God. He has power over everything, including evil. Jesus came to earth to destroy the Devil by dying on the cross. One day Jesus will return and make everything right.

**Big Picture Question:** What does Jesus have power over?

**Big Picture Answer:** Jesus has power over evil.

# Jesus Had Power Over Death

Lazarus was a friend of Jesus who lived in the village of Bethany. He lived there with his sisters, Mary and Martha. When Lazarus became very sick, Mary and Martha sent a message to Jesus: "Lord, the one You love is sick."

When Jesus heard this, He said, "This sickness will not end in death, but the Son of God will be glorified through it." But Jesus waited 2 more days before going to Bethany.

By the time Jesus got to Bethany, Lazarus had already been in the tomb 4 days. Many Jews had come to comfort Martha and Mary. As soon as Martha heard that Jesus was coming, she went to meet Him. But Mary stayed home.

Martha said to Jesus, "Lord, if You had been here, my brother wouldn't have died. But even now I know that God will give You whatever You ask."

"Your brother will rise again," Jesus told her.

Martha said, "I know that he will rise again in the resurrection at the last day."

"I am the resurrection and the life," Jesus said. "Everyone who lives and believes in Me will never die. Do you believe this?"

"Yes," she said, "I believe You are the Son of God."

Martha went back to her sister Mary and said, "The Teacher is calling for you."

Mary quickly went to Him. The Jews followed her, thinking that she was going to the tomb. Mary fell at Jesus' feet and said, "Lord, if You had been here, my brother would not have died!"

When Jesus saw her tears, and all the people with her crying, He also wept.

"Where have you put him?" Jesus asked.

The people led Jesus to the tomb. It was a cave, and a huge stone covered the opening. "Remove the stone," Jesus said.

But Martha said, "Lord, it's been four days. There will be a smell."

Jesus said, "Didn't I tell you that if you believed you would see the glory of God?"

So the stone was moved aside. Jesus raised His eyes and said, "Father, I thank You that You heard Me. Then He shouted, "Lazarus, come out!" The dead man came out, bound hand and foot with linen strips and with his face wrapped in a cloth. Jesus said, "Loose him and let him go."

**Christ Connection:** When Jesus raised Lazarus from the dead, He showed that He has power over death. Jesus said, "I am the resurrection and the life." Because Jesus died on the cross for our sin and rose from the dead, He offers eternal life to those who know and love Him.

**Big Picture Question:** Why did Jesus wait to go to Bethany?

**Big Picture Answer:** Jesus waited so that the people would know He has power over death.

# Parable of the Vineyard Workers

One day, as Jesus was teaching, He spoke to His disciples about the kingdom of heaven. He said,

"The kingdom of heaven is like a landowner who went out early in the morning to hire workers for his vineyard. He told the workers that he would pay them each one denarius (dih NER ee uhs) for the day's work. Then he sent them into his vineyard.

"The owner went out again at about nine in the morning. He saw other men standing in the marketplace doing nothing. To those men he said, 'You can also go to my vineyard, and I'll pay you whatever is right.' So off they went to work.

"At about noon, and then again at three, the owner went out and did the same thing. Then, at about five in the evening, he went and found still others standing around. He said to them, 'Why have you been standing here all day doing nothing?'

"'Because no one hired us,' the men told him.

"'You may also go to my vineyard and work,' he told them. At the end of the day, the landowner told his foreman, 'Call the workers together and give them their pay. Start with the last and end with the first.'

"When those who were hired at about five o'clock came, they each received one denarius. The men who had been hired early in the morning saw this. They thought they would get more pay, because they had worked all day. But when it was their turn, they were also paid one denarius each.

"The men began to complain to the landowner: 'These last men only worked one hour, and you paid them the same as us. We worked all day in the burning heat!'

"The landowner said, 'Friend, I have not done you wrong. Didn't you agree to work all day for a denarius? Take what is yours and go. If I want to give this last man the same as I gave you, that is my business. Are you jealous and upset because I'm generous?'

"So the last will be first, and the first last."

**Christ Connection:** Jesus' parable teaches about God's grace. God is very generous and loving. Even though we deserve to die for our sins, God gives us what we don't deserve—salvation through His Son Jesus.

**Big Picture Question:** Why did the landowner pay the last men the same amount as the first?

**Big Picture Answer:** The landowner was generous.

Once again Jesus spoke to His disciples in a parable:

"The kingdom of heaven is like a king who gave a wedding feast for his son. He sent out his slaves to tell all those who were invited to the banquet that the feast was ready. But they didn't want to come!

"The king sent out his slaves again, and said, 'Tell those who are invited: Look, I've prepared the feast. The oxen and cattle have been slaughtered, and everything is ready. Come to the wedding feast.'

"But they ignored his message again. One man went to his farm, and another went away to his business. But others grabbed the king's slaves and killed them! The king was so angry that he sent out his troops to kill those murderers and burn down their city.

"Then the king said to his slaves, 'The banquet is ready, but those who were invited are not worthy to come. So go out to where the roads leave the city and invite everyone you find to the feast.'

"So the slaves went out on the roads and gathered everyone they found—both evil men and good. The wedding feast was filled with guests. But when the king came in to see the guests, he saw a man there who was not dressed for a wedding. So the king said to him, 'Friend, how did you get in here without wedding clothes?' The man was speechless.

"Then the king told his servants, 'Tie him up hand and foot. Throw him into the outer darkness, where there will be weeping and gnashing of teeth.'

"For many are invited, but few are chosen."

**Christ Connection:** Jesus' invitation of eternal life in the kingdom of heaven is a free gift. There is nothing we can do to earn our way into heaven. Jesus did all the work when He died for our sins on the cross. When we accept the invitation, Jesus gets us ready by clothing us in His righteousness. Jesus is alive and invites us to join Him in heaven—the great wedding feast.

**Big Picture Question:** Who is invited to the kingdom of heaven?

**Big Picture Answer:** All are invited to the kingdom of heaven, but few will choose to come.

235

Jesus said, "Who is a good and faithful servant? Who will the master put in charge of all his other servants to give them their food at the right time? It will be the servant who is found working when the master comes. He is the one who will be rewarded. The master will put him in charge of all his things.

"But the wicked servant says in his heart, 'My master won't be coming back for a while.' So he starts to do all the things he knows his master will not like. He beats his fellow servants. And he eats and drinks and gets drunk, because he thinks he won't get caught.

"But there will be a day when the master will come back and the wicked servant will not be expecting him. The master will cut him to pieces and give him a place with the unbelievers. In that place there will be weeping and gnashing of teeth.

"Now, that servant who knew what his master wanted him to do, but ignored him and didn't do it, he will be severely beaten. But the servant who didn't know what his master wanted—and who did things that deserved to be punished—he will be beaten lightly.

"If someone has been given much, he will be expected to give much in return. And even more will be expected of the one who has been given more."

**Christ Connection:** Jesus is the Master who gives believers the responsibility of caring for His world and sharing the gospel. God gives gifts and talents in order to do His work. No one knows the exact time Jesus will return to earth so we must always be ready. When Jesus returns, those who faithfully worked for Him will be rewarded, but those who did not will be punished.

**Big Picture Question:** What will happen to the good and faithful servant?

**Big Picture Answer:** The good and faithful servant will be rewarded.

# Parable of the Rich Man and Lazarus

Jesus told this story to the Pharisees:

"There was a rich man who would dress in purple and fine linen. Every day he had great feasts. There was another man named Lazarus who was very poor. His body was covered with sores, and he was left at the rich man's gate. Lazarus was so hungry that he longed to eat the scraps that fell from the rich man's table. Instead, the dogs would come and lick his sores.

"One day the poor man died. He was carried away by the angels and taken to Abraham's side. The rich man also died and was buried. The rich man was sent to torment in Hades. He looked up and saw Abraham a long way off, with Lazarus at his side.

"'Father Abraham!' the rich man called out. 'Have mercy on me. I am in agony in this flame! Send Lazarus to dip the tip of his finger in water and cool my tongue.'

"'Son,' Abraham said, 'remember that during your life you had good things, just as Lazarus had bad things. Now Lazarus is comforted here, while you are in agony. Besides, there is a great space between us and you. We cannot cross over to you, and you cannot cross over to us.'

"'Father Abraham,' the rich man said, 'then I beg you to send Lazarus to my father's house. I have 5 brothers. Send Lazarus to warn them, so they won't come to this place of torment too.'

"But Abraham said, 'They have already been warned by the word of Moses and the prophets. They should listen to them.'

"'No, father Abraham,' the rich man said. 'But if someone from the dead goes to them, they will listen and change their ways.'

"But Abraham said, 'If they won't listen to Moses and the prophets, they will not listen even if someone rises from the dead.'"

**Christ Connection:** Those who receive salvation from Jesus have changed hearts—they treasure Jesus above any earthly treasure. Getting into heaven has nothing to do with who you know, what you wear, or what you do. Entering into heaven requires faith in Jesus, the Son of God. All of the Bible points us to Him.

**Big Picture Question:** Why wouldn't Abraham send Lazarus to warn the rich man's brothers?

**Big Picture Answer:** They had already been warned by Moses and the prophets.

# Parable of the Talents

Matthew 25:14-30; Luke 19:11-27

Jesus told His listeners this parable:

"It is like a man going on a journey. He called his slaves to him. To one he gave 5 talents. To another, he gave 2 talents. And to another, he gave one talent—each according to his own ability. (Now, a talent was a very large amount of money.) Then the man went on a journey.

"The man who had been given 5 talents put them to work right away and soon earned 5 more. In the same way, the man with 2 talents earned 2 more. But the man who had been given one talent went off, dug a hole in the ground, and hid his master's money.

"After a long time the master returned and asked what had happened to his money. The man who had been given 5 talents said, 'Master, you gave me 5 talents. Look, I've earned 5 more!'

'Well done, good and faithful slave!' said his master. 'You were faithful over a few things, so I will put you in charge of many things. Share your master's joy!'

"Then the man with 2 talents also came to him. He said, 'Master, you gave me 2 talents. Look, I've earned 2 more.'

'Well done, good and faithful slave!' said his master. 'You were faithful over a few things, so I will put you in charge of many things. Share your master's joy!'

"Then the man who had received one talent came and said, 'Master, I know you're a hard man. You harvest what you didn't sow and gather what you didn't plant. So I was afraid. I hid your talent in the ground. Look, you have what is yours back.'

"But his master said, 'You evil, lazy slave! If you knew that I harvest where I haven't sown and gather what I haven't planted, then you should have placed my money with the bankers. Then, I would at least have my money back with interest.'

"'Take the talent from this man and give it to the one who has 10 talents. For to everyone who has, more will be given. But from the one who does not have, even what he has will be taken away from him.

"'Now throw this good-for-nothing slave into the outer darkness, where there will be weeping and gnashing of teeth.'"

**Christ Connection:** "Well done, good and faithful slave!" Every believer, as a servant of Christ, has the task of serving God with his or her life. We eagerly wait for the day we can enter into the joy of our Master. Heaven is the eternal joy of knowing, worshipping, and enjoying Jesus.

**Big Picture Question:** Why was the master angry with the man who hid the one talent?

**Big Picture Answer:** He was angry because the man did nothing with the talent he was given.

As Jesus was setting out on a journey, a man ran up and knelt down before Him. He asked Jesus, "Good Teacher, what must I do to inherit eternal life?"

"Why do you call Me good?" Jesus asked him. "No one is good but God. You know the commandments: Do not murder. Do not commit adultery. Do not steal. Do not tell lies. Do not cheat. Honor your father and mother."

The man said to Jesus, "Teacher, I have kept all these commandments these ever since I was young."

Then, looking at him, Jesus loved him and said to him, "There is only one thing more you must do. Sell all that you have. Give it to the poor, and you will have treasure in heaven. Then come and follow Me."

After the man heard this, he went away very sad, because he was very rich.

Seeing the man's sadness, Jesus said to His disciples, "How hard it is for those who have wealth to enter the kingdom of God! It is easier for a camel to go through the eye of a needle than for a rich person to enter the kingdom of God."

The disciples asked one another, "Then who can be saved?"

Jesus said, "What is impossible with men is possible with God."

Peter said, "Look, we have left everything and followed You."

"I tell you," Jesus said, "there is no one who has left a house, wife, brothers or sisters, parents or children because of the kingdom of God, who will not receive many times more at this time, as well as eternal life in the age to come. But many who are first will be last, and the last will be first."

Then Jesus took the Twelve aside. He began to tell them about the things that would happen to Him. "Listen!" He said. "We are going up to Jerusalem. The Son of Man will be handed over to the chief priests and the scribes. They will condemn Him to death. Then they will hand Him over to the Gentiles. They will mock Him, spit on Him, and beat Him. Then they will kill Him, and He will rise on the third day."

But the disciples didn't understand what Jesus was saying.

**Christ Connection:** The rich young ruler loved his possessions more than he loved Jesus. Jesus asks us to be willing to give up everything and follow Him because He is the only one worth following. When we know and love Jesus, He is our treasure. We can let go of any treasure on earth because Jesus is better. When we follow Jesus, we follow Him into eternal life.

**Big Picture Question:** Why did the rich young ruler walk away sad?

**Big Picture Answer:** He loved his wealth and possessions more than he loved Jesus.

Six days before the Passover Feast, Jesus came to Bethany. This was the village where Lazarus lived with his sisters Mary and Martha. (Lazarus was the man Jesus had raised from the dead.) They gave a dinner for Jesus. Martha was serving them, and Lazarus was reclining at the table with Him.

Then Mary came in with an alabaster jar of pure, fragrant oil of nard—a very expensive perfume. She broke the jar and poured it over Jesus' head and feet. Then she wiped His feet with her hair. The whole house was filled with the fragrance of the oil.

Then one of His disciples, Judas Iscariot (who was about to betray Him), said, "Why wasn't this perfume sold for 300 denarii (dih NAIR i) and given to the poor?" Judas didn't say this because he cared about the poor. He said this because he was a thief. He was in charge of the disciples' money-bag and would steal part of whatever was put in it.

Jesus answered, "Leave her alone. She has done a great thing for Me. You will always have the poor with you, but you will not always have Me. By pouring this oil on My body, she has prepared Me for burial. I tell you that wherever the gospel is told in the whole world, what she has done will also be told in memory of her."

**Christ Connection:** Pouring the very expensive oil on Jesus was not a waste, it was worship. By allowing the woman to anoint Him, Jesus showed that He is more valuable than anything. Jesus knew He would soon die for sinners, be buried, and rise from the dead on the third day.

**Big Picture Question:** What did pouring the oil over Jesus do?

**Big Picture Answer:** It prepared His body for burial.

It was the time of year that the Israelites celebrated Passover. Many Israelites had traveled to Jerusalem to remember what God had done when He rescued His people from slavery in Egypt.

Jesus and His disciples traveled to Jerusalem too. When they neared Bethphage (BETH fayj) and Bethany near the Mount of Olives, Jesus sent 2 of His disciples ahead into a village.

"As soon as you enter the village," Jesus told them, "you will find a young donkey tied there. No one has ever sat on it. Untie it and bring it here to Me. If anyone says to you, 'Why are you doing this?' say, 'The Lord needs it.'"

Jesus was doing this to fulfill a prophecy by the prophet Zechariah that said the King would come, humble and gentle, and riding on a donkey.

The disciples did just as Jesus asked. They found a young donkey outside in the street. As they untied it, some people standing there said to them, "Why are you untying the donkey?"

"The Lord needs it," they said. Then they brought the donkey to Jesus and threw their robes on it. Jesus sat on the donkey.

A very large crowd had gathered. Many spread their robes on the road. Others cut branches from palm trees and spread them on the road. These were for Jesus to travel over. The crowds were praising God with joy, shouting: "The King who comes in the name of the Lord is the blessed One. Peace in heaven and glory in the highest heaven!" They knew that Jesus was their promised King.

Some of the Pharisees said to Jesus, "Teacher, tell your disciples to be quiet!"

Jesus answered, "If they didn't praise Me, the rocks would praise Me!"

When Jesus entered Jerusalem, the whole city was shaken, saying, "Who is this?" And the crowds kept saying, "This is the prophet Jesus from Nazareth in Galilee!"

**Christ Connection:** During Jesus' triumphal entry, the people welcomed Him as King. Jesus was the Messiah the prophet Zechariah spoke about: "Look, your King is coming to you; He is righteous and victorious, humble and riding on a donkey, on a colt, the foal of a donkey" (Zechariah 9:9).

**Big Picture Question:** Who did the people say Jesus was?

**Big Picture Answer:** They said He was the King who comes in the name of the Lord.

# Jesus Cleansed the Temple

Matthew 21:12-17; Mark 11:15-19; Luke 19:45-48; John 2:13-16

The Jewish Passover was near, so Jesus and His disciples went up to Jerusalem. Jesus went into the temple and found people selling oxen, sheep, and doves. He also found the money changers sitting there.

After making a whip out of cords, Jesus began to throw out all those buying and selling in the temple. He overturned the money changers' tables and the chairs of those selling doves. And He said to them, "It is written, My house will be called a house of prayer. But you have made it a den of thieves!"

The blind and the lame came to Jesus in the temple, and He healed them. The children were running and shouting, "*Hosanna* to the Son of David!"

When the chief priests and the scribes saw the wonders that Jesus did and heard the children shouting in the temple, they were very angry. They said to Him, "Do You hear what these children are saying?"

"Yes," Jesus told them. "Have you never read: You have prepared praise from the mouths of children and nursing infants?" (These words were from a psalm written by King David.)

When the chief priests and scribes heard this, they were even angrier. They started looking for a way to destroy Him. But they were also afraid of Him, because the whole crowd was amazed by His teaching.

When evening came, Jesus left and went out of the city to Bethany, where he stayed the night.

**Christ Connection:** Jesus was angry that people were misusing the temple, the place people could go to meet with God. Today, Christians do not go to a temple to meet with God or to offer sacrifices for sin. Jesus died on the cross as the final payment for sin, and we go to church to worship Him.

**Big Picture Question:** Why did Jesus chase out all those who were buying and selling in the temple?

**Big Picture Answer:** God's house—the temple—was supposed to be a place of prayer.

# The Widow's Gift

Sitting across from the temple treasury, Jesus watched how the people dropped their offerings of money into the treasury. Many rich people were putting in large amounts of money. But one poor widow came and dropped in 2 tiny coins. They were worth very little.

Jesus called to His disciples and said, "I tell you: This poor widow has put in more than all of the others. For they all gave out of their riches, but she gave everything she had. She put in all she had to live on."

**Christ Connection:** Jesus gave up everything He had in heaven to come to earth and save us from our sins. Jesus even gave up His own life, dying on the cross in our place. When you know and love Jesus, you can serve Him as the Lord of your life and offer everything you have. God takes care of His children and rewards those who seek Him.

**Big Picture Question:** Why did Jesus say that the widow had given more than all the others?

**Big Picture Answer:** She had given all she had to live on.

251

# Preparation for Passover

The Day of Unleavened Bread came when the Passover lamb had to be sacrificed. Jesus sent Peter and John, saying, "Go and prepare the Passover meal for us, so we can eat it."

"Where do You want us to prepare it?" they asked Him.

"Listen," He said to them, "go into the city. A man carrying a water jug will meet you. Follow him. Wherever he goes, tell the owner of the house, 'The Teacher asks you, "Where is the guest room where I can eat the Passover with My disciples?' He will show you a large room upstairs, furnished and ready. Make the preparations for us there."

So the disciples went into the city. They found the man and everything just as Jesus had told them, and they prepared the Passover meal.

**Christ Connection:** God's people celebrated Passover to remember when the blood of the lamb protected God's people from His wrath in Egypt. As Jesus' disciples prepared for Passover, Jesus prepared to die. In His death on the cross, Jesus made the sacrifice once and for all to take the punishment for sin. Jesus protects from God's wrath those who trust in Him.

**Big Picture Question:** Why did God's people celebrate the Passover?

**Big Picture Answer:** The Passover was to remember when the blood of the lamb protected God's people from His wrath in Egypt.

When evening came on the night of the Passover Feast, Jesus was reclining at the table with the Twelve. While they were eating, He said, "I tell you: One of you will betray Me—one who is eating with Me right now!"

The disciples were deeply troubled. They each began to say to Him, "Surely it is not I, Lord?"

"It is one of the Twelve," Jesus said. "It is the one who is dipping bread with Me in the bowl—he will betray Me. The Son of Man will go just as it is written about Him. But woe to that man who betrays the Son of Man! It would have been better for that man if he had not been born."

Then Judas, who was His betrayer, said, "Surely it is not I, Rabbi?"

"You have said it," Jesus told him.

As they were eating, Jesus took the bread, blessed and broke it. He gave it to the disciples and said, "Take and eat it. This is My body, which is given for you. Do this in remembrance of Me."

Then He took a cup and, after giving thanks, He gave it to them. They all drank from it. He said to them, "This is My blood that establishes the covenant. It is shed for many for the forgiveness of sins. But I tell you, from this moment on I will not drink of this fruit of the vine until that day when I drink it in a new way in My Father's kingdom with you."

Then, after singing psalms, they went out to the Mount of Olives.

**Christ Connection:** God loves people. In the Old Testament, God made a covenant with His people. He gave them commandments to follow so they could live in right relationship with Him. God's people broke the covenant. They didn't obey God, and they didn't love Him. Jesus made a new covenant by dying on the cross. He brought forgiveness and made the way for people to know and love God again.

**Big Picture Question:** When Jesus gave the bread to His disciples, what did He tell them to do?

**Big Picture Answer:** Jesus told them to eat it in remembrance of Him.

Jesus came with His disciples to a garden called Gethsemane (geth SEM uh nih). Leaving the other disciples, He took Peter, James, and John aside and said, "My soul is filled with sorrow. I feel as if I am dying. Wait here and stay awake with Me."

Jesus walked a little farther, then fell facedown and prayed, "Father! If it is possible, let this cup of suffering pass away from Me. But Your will be done." Jesus came back and found the disciples asleep.

"Couldn't you stay awake with Me for one hour?" He asked. Jesus went away a second and a third time to pray. Each time, He came back to find the disciples sleeping. Then He said, "Get up! My betrayer is coming."

Judas arrived with a large crowd carrying swords and clubs. Judas stepped up and kissed Jesus on the cheek—so the men would know who to arrest. When they grabbed Jesus, all His disciples ran away.

Jesus was taken to Caiaphas (KAY uh fuhs), the high priest. Caiaphas wanted a reason to kill Jesus, so he asked, "Are you the Messiah, the Son of God?"

"You have said it," Jesus answered.

The high priest said, "He has spoken against God!"

"He deserves to die!" the crowd shouted, and they spit in Jesus' face and beat Him.

At daybreak, they took Jesus to Pilate, the Roman governor. Pilate didn't think Jesus had done anything wrong, but the crowds wanted Him killed. So Pilate handed Him over to be crucified. The governor's soldiers put a scarlet robe on Him and a crown of thorns. They mocked him, saying, "Hail, King of the Jews!" Jesus was beaten and nailed to a cross. Two criminals were crucified next to Him. From noon until three in the afternoon, darkness covered the land. Then Jesus cried out, "My God, My God, why have You forsaken Me?" Then He died.

**Christ Connection:** The crucifixion and resurrection of Jesus is the center of the gospel. We deserve to die because of our sin, but Jesus died in our place. He was the blood sacrifice made once and for all for the forgiveness of sin. God was pleased with Jesus' sacrifice and raised Jesus from the dead to reign as king over all creation. We are forgiven only through Jesus (Acts 4:12).

**Big Picture Question:** What did the angel say about Jesus?

**Big Picture Answer:** The angel said that Jesus had risen, just as He said He would.

# The Emmaus Disciples

On the same day that Jesus had risen, 2 of His disciples were on their way to a village called Emmaus (ih MAY uh), which was about 7 miles from Jerusalem. They were talking about everything that had taken place. While they were talking, Jesus Himself came near and began to walk along with them—but they were kept from knowing that it was Him.

"What are you talking about?" Jesus asked.

The two men stopped walking and looked at Him. The one named Cleopas (KLEE uh puhs) said, "Are You the only person in Jerusalem who doesn't know about the things that have happened there these last few days?"

"What things?" Jesus asked.

"The things about Jesus," they said, "and how our chief priests and leaders handed Him over to be crucified. We were hoping that He was the One who would save Israel. And now, it's the third day since He was killed, and some women went early to His tomb. But they didn't find His body. They came back and said that they'd seen angels who told them Jesus was alive. Some others went to the tomb and found it empty, just as the women had said, but they didn't see Jesus."

Jesus said to them, "How slow you are to believe all that the prophets have said! Didn't the Messiah have to suffer these things?" Then, beginning with Moses and all the Prophets, Jesus taught them the many things about Himself that were written in all the Scriptures.

As they neared Emmaus, the 2 disciples asked Jesus to stay with them since it was evening. So Jesus did. As He reclined at the table with them, He took the bread, blessed and broke it, and gave it to them. At that moment, their eyes were opened! They saw that He was Jesus, but then He suddenly disappeared from their sight.

They looked at to each other and said, "Weren't our hearts on fire within us while He was explaining the Scriptures to us?"

They jumped up right away and went back to Jerusalem. They found the Eleven (for Judas was no more) and said to them, "Jesus has been raised!" Then they told the disciples all that Jesus has said on the road and how they knew He was Jesus when He broke the bread.

**Christ Connection:** The Bible is all about Jesus. When Adam and Eve sinned, God began working out His plan to send Jesus to rescue people from sin (Genesis 3:15). All of the Old Testament points forward to Jesus' life, death, and resurrection—the time when Jesus would bring God's promised salvation for sinners.

**Big Picture Question:** What did the 2 disciples do after they realized that it had been Jesus talking to them?

**Big Picture Answer:** They jumped up right away and went back to Jerusalem.

On the first day of the week in the evening, the disciples gathered together in a house. They locked the doors because they were afraid of the Jews. They didn't want to be killed as Jesus had been. Suddenly, Jesus was there, standing among them. "Peace to you!" He said.

The disciples were startled and terrified. They thought He was a ghost!

"Why are you troubled?" Jesus asked. "And why do you have doubt in your hearts? Look at My hands and My feet. It is I! Touch Me and see. A ghost doesn't have flesh and bones, like I have." Then Jesus showed them His hands and His side. So the disciples were overjoyed. It was the Lord!

They were still amazed when Jesus asked them, "Do you have anything here to eat?" So they gave Him a piece of a broiled fish, and He ate it.

Again, Jesus said to them, "Peace to you! As the Father has sent Me, I also send you." After saying this, He breathed on them and said, "Receive the Holy Spirit. If you forgive the sins of any, they are forgiven. If you do not forgive the sins of any, they are not forgiven."

Now, one of the disciples, Thomas, was not with the others when Jesus came. The other disciples kept telling him, "We have seen the Lord!"

But Thomas would not believe. "If I don't see the mark of the nails in His hands," he said, "and if I don't put my hand into His side, I will never believe!"

Eight days later, the disciples were gathered inside again. This time, Thomas was with them. Even though the doors were locked, Jesus appeared and stood among them. "Peace to you!" He said.

Then Jesus said to Thomas, "Put your finger here and touch My hands. Reach out your hand and put it into My side. Don't be an unbeliever—be a believer."

"My Lord and my God!" Thomas said.

"Because you have seen Me, you have believed," Jesus said. "Blessed are those who believe without seeing."

Over the next 40 days, Jesus appeared to many of His disciples.

**Christ Connection:** Jesus appeared to the disciples who had run away from Him just days before. The first thing He said was, "Peace to you." A normal king would have said, "Death to you." But Jesus had said, "Death to Me" when He died on the cross. Jesus can offer peace because of His death in their place.

**Big Picture Question:** Who did Jesus say was blessed?

**Big Picture Answer:** Those who believe without seeing are blessed.

Simon Peter, Thomas, Nathanael, James, John, and 2 other disciples were together at the Sea of Tiberias (ti BIHR ee uhs).

"I'm going fishing," Peter said to the others.

"We're coming with you," they told him. So they all went out and got into the boat, but that night they caught nothing.

When daybreak came, Jesus stood on the shore. The disciples, however, did not know it was Jesus.

"Men," Jesus called to them, "you don't have any fish, do you?"

"No," they answered.

"Cast the net on the right side of the boat," He told them, "and you'll find some." So they did—and their net was filled with so many fish that they couldn't even haul it in! John looked at all the fish and then at the man on the shore. "It's the Lord!" he said to Peter.

When Peter heard that it was the Lord, he dove into the sea and swam toward Jesus. But since they were not far from land (only about 100 yards away), the other disciples came in the boat, dragging the net full of fish with them. When they got to land, they saw a charcoal fire there, with fish lying on it, and bread.

"Bring some of the fish you've just caught," Jesus told them. So Peter got up and hauled the net ashore. It was full of large fish—153 of them. Even though there were so many fish, the net was not torn.

"Come and have breakfast," Jesus told them. None of the disciples dared to ask Him, "Who are You?" because they knew it was the Lord. Jesus came, took the bread, and gave it to them. He did the same with the fish.

This was now the third time Jesus appeared to the disciples after He was raised from the dead.

**Christ Connection:** When Jesus first called the disciples to follow Him, Jesus had promised to make them fishers of men—instead of catching fish, they would tell people about Jesus (Luke 5:1–11). The disciples had left Jesus when He was arrested, but Jesus still wanted to use them in God's plan to rescue people from their sin. Jesus is a Lord who forgives us and makes things right again.

**Big Picture Question:** Why did Jesus make breakfast for the disciples?

**Big Picture Answer:** He wanted to show them that the Lord forgives and makes things right again.

# Jesus Gave the Great Commission

After Jesus had been raised from the tomb, and before He returned to heaven, He gave His followers a job to do.

Jesus said to His disciples, "All authority has been given to Me in heaven and on earth. So go into all the world and preach the gospel to all people.

"Make disciples of all nations, and baptize them in the name of the Father and of the Son and of the Holy Spirit. Teach them to obey everything I have commanded you.

"Whoever believes and is baptized will be saved, but whoever does not believe will not be saved.

"And remember, I am with you always, to the end of the age."

**Christ Connection:** The good news about what Jesus has done to rescue us from our sins is too great to keep to ourselves. Before Jesus went back to heaven, He gave the disciples a job to do. Jesus wants His followers to teach people everywhere about Jesus so they will trust in Him as their Lord and Savior.

**Big Picture Question:** What does Jesus want His disciples to do?

**Big Picture Answer:** Jesus wants His disciples to go out and preach the gospel to all people.

# Jesus Ascended to Heaven

When Jesus first appeared to His disciples in that upper room, He told them not to leave Jerusalem. Instead, he told them, they were to wait for the Father's promise—the Holy Spirit.

"John baptized with water," Jesus said, "but soon you will be baptized with the Holy Spirit."

So when the disciples had come together, they asked Jesus, "Lord, are You going to restore the kingdom to Israel at this time?"

But Jesus answered, "It is not for you to know the times of things. Those are set by God by His own authority. But you will receive power when the Holy Spirit comes on you. And you will be My witnesses in Jerusalem, in all of Judea and Samaria, and to the ends of the earth."

After Jesus had said this, as they were watching, He rose up and a cloud took Him out of their sight. While He was going, they stood gazing up into heaven. Suddenly two men in white clothes (who were angels) appeared and stood beside them. They said, "Men of Galilee, why do you stand looking up into heaven? This Jesus, who has been taken from you into heaven, will come back again. He will come again in the same way you've seen Him going up into heaven."

**Christ Connection:** Jesus left earth and returned to heaven, but He did not leave us alone. Jesus promised to send the Holy Spirit to be with us and help us do God's work. One day Jesus will return to make all things new and to rule as Lord over all.

**Big Picture Question:** What did the angels say about Jesus?

**Big Picture Answer:** One day, Jesus will come back again in the same way that He left. Then He will rule as Lord over all.

On the day of Pentecost, the disciples were all gathered together in one place. Suddenly a sound like violent rushing wind came from heaven. It filled the whole house where they were staying. Then tongues, like flames of fire, appeared and rested on each one of the disciples. They were all filled with the Holy Spirit and began to speak in different languages.

Now, there were Jews living in Jerusalem. They were faithful men from every nation under heaven. When they heard these sounds, a crowd gathered. The men were confused because each one heard the disciples speaking in his own language. They were all amazed, saying to each other, "What could this be?" But some sneered and said, "They're drunk and full of wine!"

But Peter stood up, raised his voice, and said: "These people are not drunk! It's only nine in the morning. Listen to these words: This Jesus the Nazarene was a man pointed out to you by God with miracles, wonders, and signs. You used lawless people to nail Him to a cross and kill Him. But God raised Him up from the dead. It was not possible for Him to be held by death.

"God has raised Jesus from the grave. We are all witnesses of this—we have seen Him! So let all of Israel know that God has made Jesus—the One you crucified—both Lord and Messiah!"

When the people heard this, their hearts were pierced with guilt. They said to Peter and the apostles: "Brothers, what must we do to be saved?"

"Repent! Confess your sins and turn away from them," Peter said. "And each of you must be baptized in the name of Jesus Christ for the forgiveness of your sins. Then you will receive the gift of the Holy Spirit."

Those who believed Peter's message were baptized. That day about 3,000 people were added to the believers. They devoted themselves to learning all that the apostles taught. They met with other believers every day for fellowship, the breaking of bread, and prayers.

**Christ Connection:** Jesus promised to send the Holy Spirit. The coming of the Holy Spirit meant Jesus' disciples could begin their work to share the gospel with the entire world. God gives the Holy Spirit to those who trust in Jesus as Lord and Savior. The Holy Spirit gives us power to do God's work, and He changes us to be more like Jesus.

**Big Picture Question:** How did Peter say the people could be saved?

**Big Picture Answer:** People should confess their sins and turn away from them. Then they should be baptized in the name of Jesus Christ for the forgiveness of sins.

# The Church Met Needs

Acts 3:1-10; 4:32-37

*A Lame Man Is Healed*

Now Peter and John were going up together to the temple. It was three in the afternoon, the hour of prayer. There was a man there who had been lame from birth. Each day, he was carried there and placed at the temple gate called Beautiful. He would beg from those going into the temple.

When he saw Peter and John about to enter the temple, he asked for help. Peter, along with John, looked at him and said, "Look at us." So the man turned to them, expecting to get something from them.

But Peter said, "I don't have silver or gold. But I will give you what I do have. In the name of Jesus Christ, get up and walk!" Then, taking the man by the right hand, Peter raised him up. At once his feet and ankles became strong! The man jumped up, stood, and started to walk. He went into the temple with Peter and John. He was walking, leaping, and praising God.

All the people saw him, and they recognized him as the man who used to sit and beg at the Beautiful Gate. They were filled with amazement at what had happened to him.

*The Believers Share*

There was now a large group of believers, but they were all of one heart and mind. No one said that any of his things was his own, but instead they shared all that they had.

There was not a needy person among them, because all those who owned lands or houses sold them. They brought the money from the things that were sold and laid it at the apostles' feet. This was then given out for each person's needs.

Barnabas (BAHR nuh buhs)—which means Son of Encouragement—sold a field he owned. He brought the money and laid it at the apostles' feet.

**Christ Connection:** After Jesus returned to heaven, the Holy Spirit gave the disciples power to keep working. Peter healed a man who was lame with the power of Jesus' name. God changed the hearts of believers, and they shared what they had so no one was needy. God gives the Holy Spirit to believers today so the church can tell others about Jesus and show them His love.

**Big Picture Question:** How was the lame man healed?

**Big Picture Answer:** With God's power, Peter healed him in the name of Jesus.

# Seven Men Were Chosen

In those days, the number of the believers was growing. But the Greek-speaking Jews began to complain against the Hebrew-speaking Jews. The Greek-speaking Jews felt that their widows were being overlooked when the daily food was given out.

The Twelve disciples gathered all the believers together. (Now, Matthias had been chosen to replace Judas.) They said, "It isn't right for us to stop preaching about God to take care of all these daily things. So, brothers, choose 7 men to take care of this. They should be good men, who are wise and full of the Holy Spirit. They can take care of the daily business of the believers, and then we can devote ourselves to prayer and to preaching."

This sounded good to everyone. So they chose Stephen, a man full of faith and the Holy Spirit. They also chose Philip, Prochorus (PROK uh ruhs), Nicanor (ni KAY nuhr), Timon, Parmenas (PAHR mee nuhs), and Nicolaus (nik uh LAY uhs). These seven men stood before the apostles, who prayed for them and laid their hands on them.

So the preaching about God went on. It reached more and more people, and the number of the believers in Jerusalem grew greatly. Even a large group of priests became believers of the faith.

**Christ Connection:** Everyone in the church has a role in God's work. The 7 men who were chosen used their abilities to take care of others, and those who taught kept teaching the word of God. Many people heard the word of God and came to believe and trust in Jesus.

**Big Picture Question:** Why did the Twelve want men chosen to take care of the believers' problems?

**Big Picture Answer:** They wanted to keep teaching about God.

Stephen was performing great wonders and signs among the people. Then some Jews came and began to argue with Him. But they couldn't win their argument because of Stephen's wisdom and the Holy Spirit working through him.

So they gathered some men to lie about Stephen. They said he had spoken against God. The people dragged Stephen to the Sanhedrin (SAN heh drihn), which was the Jewish court. There, they told more lies against Stephen, saying, "We heard him say that Jesus will destroy this place and change the laws that Moses handed down to us."

"Is this true?" the high priest asked Stephen.

Then Stephen began to preach Jesus to them, beginning with Abraham. He reminded them of God's promises to Abraham and to Isaac. He told them about Jacob, and Joseph, and Moses. He reminded them of how God had saved the Israelite people from slavery in Egypt. Stephen spoke about the tabernacle and King David and about the temple and King Solomon.

Then Stephen looked at the Jewish leaders around him and said, "You stiff-necked people! You are always resisting the Holy Spirit—just as your fathers did. They persecuted and killed the prophets. Now you have betrayed and murdered the Righteous One—Jesus."

When the Jewish leaders heard these things, they hearts were filled with anger. But Stephen, filled by the Holy Spirit, gazed up into heaven. He said, "Look! I see the heavens opened and the Son of Man standing at the right hand of God!"

The Jewish leaders screamed at the top of their voices, covered their ears, and rushed against him. They threw Stephen out of the city and began to stone him. The witnesses laid their robes at the feet of a young man named Saul. They were stoning Stephen as he called out: "Lord Jesus, receive my spirit!" Then he knelt down and cried out with a loud voice, "Lord, do not hold this sin against them!" After saying this, Stephen died.

**Christ Connection:** Stephen was killed because he was a Christian. Jesus told His followers that they would be persecuted—hated, hurt, or even killed—for loving Him. Jesus also said that those who suffer for Him would be blessed (Matthew 5:11). We can face suffering in this life because we know great joy is waiting for us in heaven.

**Big Picture Question:** What did Stephen say about those who were stoning him?

**Big Picture Answer:** Stephen said, "Lord, do not hold this sin against them!"

# Saul on the Road to Damascus

Saul thought that stoning Stephen was the right thing to do. At that same time, a terrible persecution broke out against the church in Jerusalem. Saul wanted to destroy the church. He went into house after house, dragging off the believers—both men and women—and throwing the in prison. Many believers fled, so that they were scattered all though the land of Judea and Samaria.

Saul was given permission by the high priest to go to Damascus (duh MAS kuhs) and arrest the believers there. But while he was on his way to Damascus, a light from heaven suddenly flashed around him! Falling to the ground, he heard a voice saying, "Saul, Saul, why are you persecuting Me?"

"Who are You, Lord?" he said.

"I am Jesus," He replied. "Get up and go into the city. Then you will be told what you must do."

Saul stood up, but he was blind! So the men traveling with him took Saul by the hand and led him into Damascus. For three days he did not eat or drink.

There was a disciple in Damascus named Ananias (an uh NI uhs). The Lord said to him, "Ananias! Go to the house of Judas and ask for a man named Saul. He's praying there."

"Lord," Ananias answered, "I've heard about this man. He has harmed many of Your believers in Jerusalem, and he can arrest all those who call on Your name."

But God said, "Go! I've chosen him to take My name to Gentiles, kings, and the Israelites."

So Ananias went to Saul and placed his hands on him. At once something like scales fell from Saul's eyes, and he could see! Then he got up and was baptized. Saul immediately began preaching about Jesus in the synagogues, saying, "He is the Son of God."

Everyone who heard him was amazed. "Isn't this the man who was arresting believers?" they said.

The Jews plotted to kill Saul, but he found out. While the Jews were watching the gates, the disciples lowered Saul in a large basket through an opening in the city's wall. He escaped!

When Saul got back to Jerusalem, the disciples there were afraid of him. They didn't know he was now a believer too! But Barnabas (BAHR nuh buhs) told them Saul had changed. Saul began preaching boldly about Jesus. The Jews in Jerusalem also tried to kill him, so the disciples sent him off to Tarsus (TAHR suhs). Around this time, Saul became known as Paul.

**Christ Connection:** Jesus appeared to Saul and changed him inside and out. Jesus even changed Saul's name to Paul. Jesus called Paul, who was once an enemy to Christians, to spend the rest of his life telling people the gospel and leading them to trust Jesus and Lord and Savior.

**Big Picture Question:** What did the Lord tell Ananias that His plan for Saul was?

**Big Picture Answer:** Saul would take the good news of Jesus to Gentiles, kings, and the Israelites.

Saul—who became known as Paul—and Barnabas (BAHR nuh buhs) were sent out by the Holy Spirit to teach the good news of Jesus. They preached all across the island of Cyprus (SI pruhs). Then they returned to the mainland and went to the city of Antioch.

On the Sabbath, they went into the synagogue where Paul began to preach the message of Jesus. When he had finished, the people begged him to come again on the following Sabbath and tell them more.

On the following Sabbath, almost the whole town gathered to hear the message of the Lord. But when the Jews saw the crowds, they were filled with jealousy and began to insult what Paul was saying.

Then Paul and Barnabas boldly said: "We had to give God's message to you first. But since you reject it, we now turn to the Gentiles!

When the Gentiles heard this, they rejoiced and many became believers. But the Jews stirred up trouble for Paul and Barnabas until they had to leave Antioch.

They next went to Iconium (i KOH nee uhm)—and the same thing happened there. They spoke in the synagogue in such a way that many Jews and Greeks believed. But the Jews who refused to believe stirred up the people against them. There was a plot to kill Paul and Barnabas, but they escaped.

Then they traveled to Lystra (LIS truh) where Paul healed a lame man. When the crowds saw what Paul had done, they began praising Paul and Barnabas as gods. Paul and Barnabas heard this and tore their robes, shouting: "No! We are men, just like you. We want to tell you the good news of God."

Then some Jews came from Antioch and Iconium and turned the people against Paul and Barnabas. They stoned Paul and dragged him out of the city, thinking he was dead. But Paul got up, and the next day he and Barnabas went to Derbe.

In Derbe, they made many disciples. Then they returned to Lystra and to Iconium, encouraging the believers there to continue in the faith.

After that, they gathered with the church at Antioch and reported everything God had done with them and how He had opened the door of faith to the Gentiles.

**Christ Connection:** Paul obeyed the Great Commission to tell the world about Jesus. Many of the Jews rejected Christ, so Paul shared the gospel with the non-Jews. Many of them believed in Jesus. God uses people to tell others about Jesus so that people all over the world can be saved from their sin by trusting in Jesus as Lord and Savior.

**Big Picture Question:** Why did Paul and Barnabas go on their journeys?

**Big Picture Answer:** They went to preach the good news of Jesus.

Paul and Silas went back to visit all the towns in which Paul had preached God's message in his first journey. He wanted to see how the believers were doing.

They traveled to Lystra (LIS truh), and from there went on to the city of Philippi (fuh LIP i). On the Sabbath day, they went outside the city gate by the river, to a place of prayer. They sat down and spoke to the women gathered there. A woman named Lydia, who was a dealer in purple cloth, was listening. The Lord opened her heart to Paul's words, and she and all her household were baptized. Then she invited Paul and the others to say at her house.

One day, as they were on their way to prayer, they met a slave girl who was possessed by a spirit. The spirit made her able to tell fortunes, and she made a lot of money for her owners. She followed Paul and the others for many days. Paul was greatly annoyed and ordered the spirit to come out of her. And it came out right away.

But the girl's owners were furious! Since she could no longer tell fortunes, they couldn't make any money off her. They dragged Paul and Silas to the authorities. A mob joined in the attack against them, and the chief magistrate ordered them to be beaten with rods. Then they were thrown into jail and their feet were chained in the stocks.

About midnight Paul and Silas were praying and singing songs to God, and the other prisoners were listening to them. Suddenly, there was a violent earthquake that shook the foundations of the jail. All the doors flew open, and everyone's chains came loose! When the jailer woke up and saw the prison doors open, he drew his sword and was about to kill himself, because he thought the prisoners had escaped.

But Paul called out, "Don't hurt yourself! We are all here!"

Then the jailer rushed in and fell down trembling before Paul and Silas. "Sirs," he said, "what must I do to be saved?"

So they said, "Believe on the Lord Jesus, and you will be saved—you and your household." The jailor took them that night and washed their wounds. Right away he and all his family were baptized. He brought them into his house and fed them. Later that day, Paul and Silas were set free.

**Christ Connection:** The jailer was saved because he believed in Jesus. Jesus offers us salvation as a gift. He did all the work to save us by dying on the cross. We do not need to earn salvation; we just need to receive it by believing in Jesus.

**Big Picture Question:** What did Paul and Silas do while they were in prison?

**Big Picture Answer:** They prayed and sang songs to God.

# Paul Preached in Europe

Paul and Silas traveled to Thessalonica (thes uh lok NI kah) and began preaching in the synagogue about Jesus. Some of the Jews and Greeks there became believers, but others wanted to attack Paul and Silas. They escaped and went to Berea where the same thing happened. The believers then sent Paul to Athens. Paul sent word for Silas and Timothy to come to him as soon as possible.

While Paul was waiting for them in Athens, he saw that the city was full of idols. So he began teaching about Jesus in the synagogue and in the marketplace every day to those who happened to be there.

Some of the people brought him to the Areopagus (air ee OP uh guhs). This was a sort of meeting place where people gathered to talk about thoughts and ideas. The people said, "We want to learn more about this new teaching."

So Paul stood in the middle of the Areopagus and said: "Men of Athens! I see that you are very religious. I even found an altar with these words written on it:

*TO AN UNKNOWN GOD.*

I tell you that your "unknown god" is the God who made the world and everything in it. He is Lord of heaven and earth. He doesn't live in shrines made by human hands. He Himself gives everyone life and breath. The Lord God now commands all people everywhere to turn away from their sins. The day is coming when He will judge the world. God has given us proof of this by raising His Son Jesus from the dead."

When they heard about being raised from the dead, some began to making fun of Paul. Others said, "We'd like to hear from you again about this." But some became believers.

After this, Paul left Athens and went to Corinth. There he met a Jewish man named Aquila (AK wih luh) and his wife Priscilla. They had just come to Italy because Claudius had ordered all the Jews to leave Rome. They were tentmakers, and—since Paul was a tentmaker—he stayed and worked with them. On the Sabbath days, Paul went to the synagogues and to preach.

Paul stayed there a year and 6 months, teaching the word of God. After that, Paul said good-bye and sailed away to Syria. Priscilla and Aquila went with him.

**Christ Connection:** The men of Athens worshipped a false god whom they did not know. Paul explained to the men God's plan of salvation. He said that only God should be worshipped. Paul talked about Jesus and the resurrection. People can know God because Jesus took the punishment for sin that separates people from God.

**Big Picture Question:** Who did Paul tell the people of Athens that the "unknown god" was?

**Big Picture Answer:** The "unknown god" was really the Lord God who made the world and everything in it.

Paul traveled from place to place, teaching about Jesus. At Ephesus (EF uh suhs), God performed extraordinary miracles by Paul's hands. Even facecloths or work aprons that had touched Paul's skin were brought to the sick and they were healed, and the evil spirits came out of them.

During that time there was a silversmith named Demetrius, who made silver shrines for the false god Artemis. He and the other craftsman were losing money. They blamed Paul and the other believers, because the people were turning to God and didn't need shrines for false gods. They started a riot and even grabbed up two of Paul's traveling companions. Paul wanted to go to them, but the disciples wouldn't let him—they were afraid he would be killed! The city clerk calmed the crowd down and said, "Men of Ephesus! If Demetrius and the craftsmen have a case against anyone, the courts are in session. Let them bring charges against one another." Then the crowds went away.

After the uproar was over, Paul left Ephesus. In the city of Troas (TROH as), on the first day of the week, Paul spoke to the people. Since he was leaving the next day, his message went on until midnight. There was a young man named Eutychus (YOO tuh kuhs), who was sitting on a window sill. He sank into a deep sleep and fell down from the third story and died. But Paul went down, embraced him, and said, "Don't be alarmed, for his life is in him!" The boy was brought home alive, and the people were greatly comforted.

Paul left Troas and traveled back to Ephesus. There he spoke to the elders of the church once more and prayed with all of them. There was a great deal of weeping, because everyone knew this might be the last time they saw Paul.

Paul then wanted to go to Jerusalem, and he set sail to begin the journey back there. Along the way, the Holy Spirit warned Paul not to go to Jerusalem, but he kept going. A little later, a prophet from Judea came to Paul. He took Paul's belt and tied his own feet and hands. He said, "This is what the Holy Spirit says: 'In this way the Jews in Jerusalem will bind the man who owns this belt and deliver him into Gentile hands.'" The people begged Paul not to go up to Jerusalem, but he would not listen.

**Christ Connection:** Paul shared the gospel with people who didn't know Jesus, and he encouraged believers in the church to keep loving Jesus. As people heard the message of salvation, God changed their hearts, and they turned away from their sin. The good news about Jesus is powerful and life-giving.

**Big Picture Question:** What happened to Eutychus?

**Big Picture Answer:** He fell out of a window and died. But Paul—with God's power—brought him back to life.

When Paul reached Jerusalem, he went to the temple. Some Jews saw him there and stirred up the crowd against him. They accused him of teaching things that were against God. They grabbed Paul and dragged him out of the temple.

As they were trying to kill him, the Roman army commander stopped them and arrested Paul. As he was taking Paul back to the army barracks, Paul asked to speak to the people. He spoke to them in Hebrew, and he told about how he used to arrest the believers and throw them into jail. Then he told them all about how he had come to believe in Jesus Christ. And last, he told them how God had sent him to preach to the Gentiles.

At this, the crowd shouted, "Wipe this person off the earth—it's a disgrace for him to live!"

The commander took Paul inside the barracks. The next night, the Lord appeared to Paul and said, "Have courage! You have taught about Me in Jerusalem, so you must also teach about me in Rome."

The Jews plotted to kill Paul, but Paul's nephew heard about the plot and told the Roman commander. The soldiers slipped Paul out at night took him to the governor. Paul was held there for two years, before he was sent to Rome. (Because Paul was a Roman citizen, he could demand to be heard by the Roman Caesar.)

Paul set sail for Italy on a boat filled with prisoners like himself. But it was a dangerous time of year to sail, and the ship was soon hit by a terrible storm. The ship wrecked near an island called Malta. Paul and all the others had to swim to shore.

Now the leading man of the island was named Publius (PUHB lee uhs). His father was very sick. Paul went to him, and after praying, he healed him. After this, all those on the island who had diseases also came and were cured. When it was time for Paul and the others to leave, the islanders gave them everything they needed.

At last, Paul reached Rome. He was still a prisoner, but he was allowed to stay in a house by himself with a guard. Paul stayed in Rome for two years in his own rented house. He taught all who visited him about the kingdom of God and the Lord Jesus Christ.

**Christ Connection:** Paul's work to spread the good news of Jesus continued in Rome. No punishment or suffering kept Paul from telling others about Jesus. The Holy Spirit gives believers power to share the gospel all over the world so people will know and love Jesus.

**Big Picture Question:** What did the Lord say when he appeared to Paul?

**Big Picture Answer:** The Lord said, "Have courage! You have taught about Me in Jerusalem, so you must also teach about me in Rome."

Paul wrote a letter to the church at Corinth, telling them many things about how to follow Jesus.

### Running the Race

Paul said that living the Christian life was like running a race. He said: "Don't you know that all the runners race, but only one receives the prize? You must run to win. You aren't running for a crown that will fade away. You are running for an eternal crown in heaven."

### The Lord's Supper

Paul reminded the church of Jesus' words at the last supper. Paul said, "On the night when He was betrayed, the Lord Jesus took bread, gave thanks, broke it, and said, 'This is My body. Eat this in remembrance of Me.' In the same way, after supper He also took the cup and said, 'This cup is the new covenant established by My blood. Drink this in remembrance of Me.'"

### Spiritual Gifts

"There are many different gifts and ministries," Paul wrote, "but they all come from the Lord. Some have the gift of wisdom, some have knowledge, and others have the gift of faith. Still others might have the gift of languages or prophecy. But all are gifts from God, and they are given to each person as He chooses."

### Love

Paul said everything must be done in love. "Love is patient, love is kind. Love does not envy, is not boastful, is not conceited, does not act improperly, is not selfish, is not provoked, and does not keep a record of wrongs. Love finds no joy in unrighteousness but rejoices in the truth. It bears all things, believes all things, hopes all things, endures all things. Love never ends."

Finally, Paul wrote: "Be alert and stand strong in the faith. Your every action must be done with love."

**Christ Connection:** Jesus' mission for the church is for believers to come together to worship God and share the gospel.

**Big Picture Question:** What did Paul say living the Christian life was like?

**Big Picture Answer:** Paul said that living the Christian life was like running a race.

Some people were saying the Day of the Lord's judgment had already come. But Paul wrote this letter to the church of the Thessalonians. In it, he explained that this was not true. Paul told the believers that no one knows exactly when Jesus is coming back, except God Himself.

Paul encouraged the believers to stand strong in their faith. He wrote to them, saying, "From the beginning, God chose to save you." Then Paul prayed for them: "May our Lord Jesus Christ Himself and God our Father encourage your hearts and strengthen you in every good work and word."

Paul also asked the church to pray for him and his fellow teachers: "Pray that the Lord's message may spread quickly, and that it will be honored. The Lord is faithful. He will strengthen and guard you from the evil one."

Paul warned against those who were lazy and did not work as they should. He wrote, "If anyone isn't willing to work, he should not eat." This was because Paul had heard that some people were not only not working themselves, but they were also messing up the work of others."

Paul ended his letter by saying: "May the Lord of peace Himself give you peace always in every way. The Lord be with all of you."

**Christ Connection:** No one knows when Jesus will return, but Christians should be ready for Him. When Jesus returns, unbelievers will be punished for their sin and those who trust Jesus as Lord and Savior will be saved.

**Big Picture Question:** When is the Jesus coming back?

**Big Picture Answer:** No one knows when Jesus is coming back except God Himself.

# God's Warning to Seven Churches

John saw a vision of heaven, and he wrote down all the things he saw and sent it to the 7 churches—just as the Lord told him to do.

*The Letter to Ephesus (EF uh suhs):*
"I know your good works and that you cannot stand evil. But this is what I have against you: You have forgotten your love for the Lord. Remember how you were when you first believed. Turn back to Me and do the works you did at first."

*The Letter to Smyrna:*
"I know your poverty. I know there are those who tell lies about you. Don't be afraid of what you are about to suffer. Look, the Devil is about to throw some of you into prison to test you. Be faithful until your death, and I will give you the crown of life."

*The Letter to Pergamum (PUHR guh muhm):*
"I know you live in a place where it is hard to worship God. It is where Satan's throne is! But you hold on to My name, and you do not deny your faith in Me."

*The Letter to Thyatira (thi uh TI ruh):*
"The Son of God says: I know your works—your love, faithfulness, service, and endurance. But I have this against you: You put up with sin. You do not punish it."

*The Letter to Sardis:*
"I know your works. You have a reputation for being alive, but you are dead. Your works are not completed before God. If you are not alert, I will come like a thief."

*The Letter to Philadelphia:*
"I know your works. You have kept My word and have not denied My name. So I have placed before you an open door that no one is able to close—that is, heaven. I am coming quickly. Hold on to what you have, so that no one takes your crown.

*The Letter to Laodicea (lay oh duh SEE uh):*
"I know your works. You are neither cold nor hot. So, because you are lukewarm, I am going to vomit you out of My mouth. So repent. Listen! I stand at the door and knock. If anyone hears My voice and opens the door, I will come in to him and have dinner with him, and he with Me."

**Christ Connection:** Jesus loves the church. His message to 7 local churches called them to turn away from their sin and remain faithful to Him. Jesus is a Savior who saves sinners and is changing them to be like Him.

**Big Picture Question:** What will Jesus do for those who hear His voice and open the doors of their hearts to Him?

**Big Picture Answer:** Jesus will come in to those people.

In John's vision of heaven, he also saw the things that would happen when Jesus comes back to earth again. John said:

"I saw heaven opened, and there was a white horse. Its rider is called Faithful and True. His eyes were like a fiery flame, and there were many crowns on His head. He wore a robe stained with blood, and His name is the Word of God. The armies that were in heaven followed Him on white horses, wearing pure white linen. And He has a name written on His robe and on His thigh:

*KING OF KINGS*
*AND LORD OF LORDS.*

"Then I saw the beast, the kings of the earth, and their armies gathered together to wage war against the rider and against His army. But the beast was taken prisoner, and along with him the false prophet. Both of them were thrown into the lake of fire.

"Then I saw a new heaven and a new earth. I also saw the Holy City, a new Jerusalem, coming down out of heaven from God. I heard a loud voice from the throne, saying,

*'Look! God will live with man. They will be His people, and He will be their God. He will wipe away every tear from their eyes. Death will no longer exist. Sadness, crying, and pain will no longer exist. These things have passed away.'*

"Then one of the angels came and carried me away to a great and high mountain. He showed me the holy city of Jerusalem. The city had a high wall, with 12 gates. The wall was made of jasper, and each gate was made of a single pearl. The foundations of the wall were decorated with every kind of precious stone: jasper, sapphire, chalcedony, emerald, sardonyx, carnelian, chrysolite, beryl, topaz, chrysoprase, jacinth, and amethyst. And the street of the city was pure gold, like clear glass.

"The city does not need the sun or the moon to shine on it. God's glory is its light, and its lamp is the Lamb. Night will no longer exist, and people will not need lamplight or sunlight, because the Lord God will give them light. And they will reign forever and ever."

**Christ Connection:** Jesus promised to come back to earth soon. When Christ returns, those who know and love Jesus will be with Him and enjoy Him forever. God will undo every bad thing caused by sin—no more death, no more pain, no more tears. Jesus will make all things new.

**Big Picture Question:** Why will there be no need for a lamp in heaven?

**Big Picture Answer:** God's glory will be its light and there will be no more night.

295

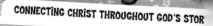

**THE**

# BIG PICTURE
## INTERACTIVE BIBLE

WATCH THE BIBLE
COME TO LIFE
**DOWNLOAD
FREE
AUGMENTED
REALITY APP**

FEATURING THE
**GOSPEL
PROJECT**
FOR KIDS

CONNECTING CHRIST THROUGHOUT GOD'S STORY

**THE**

# BIG PICTURE
## OF WHAT GOD
## HAS ALWAYS WANTED

CHARLES F. BOYD

Illustrations by
Heath McPherson

FEATURING THE
**GOSPEL
PROJECT**
FOR KIDS

CONNECTING CHRIST THROUGHOUT GOD'S STOR

### The Big Picture Interactive Bible
*March 1, 2014*

Featuring full-color, fully designed pages that include call-out sections, plus a free downloadable app that brings the dazzling images to life and provides narration, this Bible meets kids in the visual world to which they are so accustomed today.

### The Big Picture of What God Has Always Wanted
*October 1, 2013*

More than a children's book, *The Big Picture of What God Has Always Wanted* is for parents who care deeply about passing on a legacy of faith in Christ to the next generation—parents who invite children to "ask Jesus into your heart."

### The Big Picture: Making God the Focus of Your Life
*September 1, 2013*

Best-selling young adult authors Hayley and Michael DiMarco help teenagers become more aware of God's presence with them today and forever, giving them a "big picture" look at what life is really all about.

PARENT Connection
B&H KIDS

BH KIDS
EVERY *little* WORD MATTERS
BHKidsBuzz.com

THE BIG PICTURE
MAKING GOD THE MAIN FOCUS OF YOUR LIFE
HAYLEY & MICHAEL DiMARCO

# Visit us online.

## Helping kids know Christ... Empowering parents to be the guide.

**B&H KIDS**

search here ...

follow us on twitter | facebook | more from B&H

Parent Connection | Resources | About Us | Digital Resources | Levels of Biblical Learning | Contact Us

### Our Mission

B&H KIDS creates Bible-centered, age appropriate, engaging content for kids.

Our resources are designed to help kids develop a lifelong relationship with Jesus and to empower parents to guide them in their spiritual growth.

**B&H KIDS** is the children's imprint of B&H Publishing Group, a division of LifeWay Christian Resources. We launched this imprint in 2012 to focus on Bible-based books and products for kids, with a strong commitment to fun and innovative content and tools to engage children.

As an ongoing emphasis of design and development, these products are especially geared to help parents and leaders interact with kids in ways that truly make an impact—and a powerful difference in their lives. We're working diligently to make sure everything we create empowers parents, teachers, pastors, and others who love children to help them grow in their Christian faith.

Parent Connection | Resources | About Us | Digital Resources | Levels of Biblical Learning | Contact Us

Scan this or type that

**kids.bhpublishinggroup.com/about-us**

PARENT Connection
B&H KIDS

**B&H KIDS**

**EVERY little WORD MATTERS™**
BHKidsBuzz.com

# What is Parent Connection?

Each **Parent Connection** feature offers a key Bible verse or passage related to the book's content, activities tied to the book's theme, life application points (for teens), and family discussion questions. Beyond simply reading, parents and kids will create memories together while learning valuable life lessons.